ACTIVISTS AND NONACTIVISTS:

A Psychological Study of American College Students

Larry C. Kerpelman, Ph.D.

Department of Psychology
University of Massachusetts
Amherst, Massachusetts

Behavioral Publications, Inc.   1972   New York

Library of Congress Catalog Card Number 78-174273

Standard Book Number 87705-065-1

BEHAVIORAL PUBLICATIONS, 2852 Broadway—
Morningside Heights, New York, New York 10025

Printed in the United States of America

For Joan

Social Problems Series

Sheldon R. Roen, Ph.D., Editor

CONTENTS

FOREWORD

The last half dozen years have made most of us observers of the students on the campuses of this nation. Peter Schrag called this the new national fad: student watching.

There were, so far as I know, no serious predictions in the late '50's and early '60's that colleges and universities were close to a serious conflict with students over the purposes and the uses and governance of universities, and on the brink of grave disagreements over the techniques of controversy, to mention just two sets of problems. The hostility and resentment that characterized this period come as a surprise to professionals and amateurs alike.

After events on the campuses began to attract attention, this deficiency in information was made up with impressive speed. We went from no theory at all to more explanations than we needed. All aspects of the entire complex phenomenon were overdetermined. With all of the plausible explanations now readily available, the wonder is that we had, nevertheless, little or no warning.

Yet as a close observer and participant, I was never very comfortable with the state of observation and theorizing. For one thing, many of the generalizations were obviously less universal than proposed. The samples were limited, and much of the data was anecdotal and unsystematically collected. They often reflected the wishes, fears, and, in some cases, the ideological position of the observer. The liberal observer saw the student activist as enlightened, able, idealistic. The conservative saw him as frivolous, undisciplined, self right-eous. Each could find data to support his view.

A second concern to the practitioner was that the analyses were of so little use in choosing among alternative policies. Speculations about the effects of Dr. Spock were interesting, may even have had some validity, but did not lead easily to derivations about the most effective means to restore a sense of community to a troubled campus.

And now as I write this, the Fall of 1971, we find our campuses in, at least by contrast with five years ago, a tranquil state. Some have observed this with some anxiety, as if waiting for another shoe to drop. I believe a posture of caution is intelligent precisely because of the situation I have described. If one were to take as valid just half the explanations that were given for the turbulence, and then examine the conditions that were by those theories alleged to be causal, one would conclude not that we would be in repose but rather that we would be in turmoil for at least another decade. When knowledge and theory are in such a primitive state, a wise man is cautious.

Neither I nor, I suspect, my young colleague who wrote this book would argue that this modest research effort solves the general problem that I have outlined. But it is a good example of the kind of painstaking work that needs to be done. The experienced reader cannot help but be bemused by the number of times the author's hardnosed data run counter to much prevailing rhetoric. Whether his findings turn out to be more descriptive in general than the rhetoric is less important than the fact that the effort is being made to use the best methodology and design to answer serious questions. I am pleased to support Dr. Kerpelman's argument for more work of this kind.

All experienced investigators know how difficult it is to do this kind of research. It is obvious that the educational system must make it easier. A firm commitment to systematic efforts such as this one, to learn more about our students' attitudes, interests, and abilities, will help to make our institutions more useful and, hopefully, more rewarding places for all members of the campus community.

GER W. HEYNS
1 Arbor, Michigan

Dr. Kerpelman received his A.B. in psychology from the Johns Hopkins University in 1958 and his Ph.D. in psychology from the University of Rochester in 1963. He has been associated with the Institute for Juvenile Research, the University of Illinois College of Medicine, and the University of Massachusetts. Dr. Kerpelman is the author of numerous articles that have been published in a variety of periodicals, including the *Journal of Counseling Psychology*, the *Journal of Experimental Psychology, Child Development*, and *Educational and Psychological Measurement*.

PREFACE

The United States in the 1960's witnessed the metamorphosis of its college generations from apathetic caterpillars into active butterflies. With that emergence came attempts on the part of psychologists, sociologists, political scientists, educators, social commentators, and others to understand and to explain this new youth movement. As we enter the 1970's, hypotheses and speculations abound, and yet our real knowledge of the determinants of student activism is sparse. Is it because the movement changes so rapidly that we no sooner "explain" it than it becomes different, is it because we tend to speculate from the armchair rather than examine in the field, is it because we have asked the wrong questions, or is it because we have asked the right questions in the wrong way? Many researchers would argue that the first alternative is true, others would agree with the second, many student activists would themselves answer the third question affirmatively, and a small minority of investigators would side with the fourth. My own opinion, as is made increasingly clear throughout this book, is that all of these questions are on target. It was my multiple dissatisfactions with the so-called "explanations" of student activism that stimulated me to begin the research that culminated in this book. Put in a more positive way, I wanted to obtain a better understanding of an interesting and important social phenomenon.

My own philosophy, or working model of human behavior,

if you will, is that any human action takes place within a context of social, political, economic, and moral factors, but that this contextual net is ultimately funneled through the sum total of the individual person's past learnings and experiences—his personality—to emerge as overt behavior. I see student activism in the same light.

It should not be surprising that a psychologist should view behavior—no matter what its stimuli—as filtered through personality. And it should not be surprising that a psychologist should choose to examine psychological factors, just as the sociologist chooses to examine social factors, the political scientist, political events, and so on. As I have indicated in the last chapter of this book, diverse elements like these must be taken into account in order to fully comprehend any social movement, much less one as volatile and as complex as student activism. But the world is more complicated than it was in da Vinci's day, and it is the rare one among us who can encompass, comprehend, and integrate all of these approaches and come up with the "complete" picture of a social phenomenon. Certainly I am not one of those exceptions; this book is an attempt to examine one contributory aspect of activism (and non-activism). I hope I have done so in as meaningful, yet precise, a fashion as possible.

I hope that this book's appeal will be to all those who are vitally interested in college students: psychologists, sociologists, political scientists, educators, university and college administrators, counseling and guidance personnel, journalists, and students themselves. I have written it so that both the scientifically inclined reader and the informed layman can read it with profit. For the sake of the latter, the technical fine points of methodology and statistical treatment of the data have been confined primarily to one chapter, Chapter 4, which can be skipped without losing the essential thread of the book.

The research on which this book is based was made possible through receipt of a research grant, number OEG 1-8-08AO28-0032-058 from the U.S. Office of Education, Department of Health, Education, and Welfare. The opinions expressed herein do not necessarily reflect the policy of the U.S. Office of Education, and no official endorsement by that Office should be inferred. The grant technical report, of which this book is a much-expanded and revised version, is available from the Educational Resources Information Center Document Reproduction Service as document number ED-038-946. The writing of this book was made possible through receipt of a grant for the Summer of 1970 from the University of Massachusetts Graduate Research Council. I thank these sources for their support.

I also acknowledge the help of many people who assisted me in many important ways with this project. Charlene Doyle and Jean Ann Pezzoli served as my able research assistants, and Rinda Iascone and Elaine Youngblood provided extremely efficient and competent secretarial services in preparing the manuscript. Kenneth Purcell and Jeanne Phillips gave me personal encouragement and administrative support for the writing of this book. I was fortunate to have, on each campus at which this research was conducted, a consultant who served as a liaison person with the student organizations involved and who helped coordinate the myriad details requisite to administration of the research procedures at each institution. Because I have promised anonymity to the institutions that participated in this research, the consultants must remain unnamed. Likewise, the students who participated in this research are anonymous, even to me, but without their cooperation, this study could not have been conducted. I owe them my deep gratitude: I hope this book will say something to them.

Finally, I want to acknowledge the contributions of my wife, Joan Kerpelman. She had to spend many evenings alone while I was involved in this project and wrote this book, and yet she could still retain enough objectivity about it to type parts of earlier drafts, to read and comment upon them, and to give me meaningful advice. In these tangible ways, and in other ways not so tangible, she helped this book come into being.

Larry C. Kerpelman
Amherst, Massachusetts

1 / COLLEGE STUDENT ACTIVISM

American higher education has witnessed, since the early 1960's, the emergence of its students from apathy to activism. The college students of the 1950's were noted for their almost exclusive interest in vocational and personal security. The students of the Sixties, on the other hand, were noted for their apparent disinterest in these goals and their expressed concern, instead, for social justice, interpersonal sincerity, and genuine morality. Some serious observers (e.g., Bettelheim, 1969; Kennan, 1968) have viewed this development with skepticism or disdain, while others (e.g., Bay, 1967; Flacks, 1967) have welcomed or embraced it. No matter what the range of sympathies of observers of the youth scene toward the direction (real or imagined) being taken by today's student generation is, it is readily apparent that the issue engenders curiosity and interest among students themselves, college faculty, administrators at institutions of higher education, governmental officials, social scientists, journalists, and the public at large.

Although several writers (Astin, 1968; Braungart, 1966; Peterson, 1968c) have indicated that activist students are a minority of the entire U.S. college population, it also has been suggested that this "prophetic minority" (Newfield, 1966) frequently engages the sympathy and participation of a larger part of the student population (Peterson, 1968c). Furthermore, activist students are a growing force for change in American higher education and in American society as a

1

whole. In a national survey, Peterson (1968b) chronicled an increased activism between 1965 and 1968 aimed toward a larger student role in campus governance, as well as a doubling, in the same interval, of the number of campuses experiencing organized student protest of the Vietnam War. As we begin the 1970's, it becomes increasingly important for us to attempt to gain a better understanding of America's college students and the student activism movement.

Recent developments attest to an interest in gaining an objective understanding of the factors that underlie student activism. A group of eminent scholars at the Center for Advanced Study in the Behavioral Sciences recently put forth a call for a more comprehensive and objective survey of the determinants of student activism than had heretofore been done. Their statement read, in part:

> The answers to . . . questions related to student activism are just not known at present. It is obvious that this phenomenon is importantly affecting university structure and function. It is also obvious that it is receiving a tremendous amount of attention and reaction. Because of this importance and visibility it deserves the kind of comprehensive examination that can provide insights into the behavioral aspects of the phenomenon [Fellows at the Center for Advanced Study in the Behavioral Sciences, 1968, pp. 22-23].

Occurring almost simultaneously with that statement was the initiation by the American Council on Education of a large research project to study the institutional and personal background variables related to college student activism (Astin, 1968). Another development has been the establishment, also under the aegis of the American Council on Education, of a Special Committee on Campus Tensions. The establishment, in 1970, of the President's Commission on Campus Unrest is perhaps the most widely known development. Most of these endeavors are still underway, or they have been reported only in preliminary form. They have been supplemented by reports in the social science literature of research investigations, more limited in scope, on student social and political activism. Of course, over and above these empirical approaches, numerous speculative analyses and reports on the "movement" have appeared in the mass media and the underground press.

Yet, for all that has been written, much confusion and lack of knowledge remain concerning the personal and environmental determinants of student sociopolitical activism. The reasons for this state of affairs are several. To begin, much of the material written has been highly conjectural. Broad social trends have been discussed, social philosophy has been delved into, and hypotheses about the developmental backgrounds of students have been entertained, but precious little direct empirical evidence has been obtained (see, as examples of this speculative approach, Bettelheim, 1969; Halleck, 1968; Kennan, 1968; Sampson, 1967). This state of affairs has moved one writer to observe, rather poetically, "Interpretations of the radical movement and its meaning . . . exist in great and wonderful profusion [Peterson, 1968b, p. 3]." Compared to the tide of conjecture and uncontrolled observation, the number of studies reporting objective data on college student activists is small. The author would echo Astin's remarks:

> . . . most of the published material has been of a journalistic and speculative nature representing, for the most part, anecdotal accounts of confrontations on specific campuses or speculative analyses of the protest movement. While such writings have provided a wealth of provocative hypotheses concerning student activism, they offer little empirical information concerning the personal and social determinants of student activism [Astin, 1968, p. 149].

The paucity of empirical efforts in this field is easy to understand. The practical problems involved in obtaining student and institutional cooperation, in being on, or traveling to, campuses where activism is "hot," and the numerous conceptual and methodological difficulties enumerated below are a few of the more obvious obstacles to empirical research on the determinants of student activism.

Psychological Investigations of Activism

To be sure, empirical research on student activism has been undertaken, and selective reviews of this research have been published elsewhere (cf. Bay, 1967; Block, Haan, and Smith, 1968; Katz, 1967). Unfortunately, these reviews have tended to accept uncritically the conclusions of the various investigators, considering neither the problems in experimental design, the tenuous connections that are frequently made between data and conclusions, nor the overgeneralizations that have so often occurred in the research literature. It is beyond the scope of this book, though, to present as complete a critical analysis of the activism research as it deserves. What follows in this section instead is a review that is limited to three aims. First, it attempts to illustrate certain consistent problems that have occurred in efforts to investigate student activists' backgrounds and personality characteristics. Some of these problems are so consistent that they may even appear, at first glance, to be inherent in investigation of the phenomenon itself. Second, the review that follows aims to document the comparatively small return of substantive knowledge that has resulted from this research relative to the effort that has been expended. For so important a social trend, this is indeed unfortunate. Third, it hopes to provide a general basis for suggesting hypotheses and conceptual refinements, and to provide the specific basis for the thinking that went into the design for the invootigation that is reported subsequently in this book.

Before going on, I should remark that the weaknesses inherent in previous research on student social and political activism are, in good measure, inherent in the study of any social movement as volatile, as changing, and as much a part of the social fabric as is this phenomenon. Many of the oft-cited studies of the activism "movement" were undertaken in the early 1960's, when the movement was in its infancy, and when the techniques and instruments available to study it were in a similarly unrefined state. Any review of the previous research should be considered with these difficulties in mind.

Confounding activism and ideology

Part of the problem in many activism research efforts has been due to the nearly universal confusion (or, as it is more technically termed, confounding) of political activism and political ideology that has occurred among those who study and speak of student activism. Almost invariably, characteristics have been imputed to "student activists" when the students studied or speculated about have been ideologically *left* on the political spectrum. The conclusions that have been reached may well be true of otudento oubcumod under the heading of left activists, but it is impossible to tell whether the characteristics found to be associated with that particular subgroup are a function of their political activism, their left-wing political ideology, or a combination of the two. As Cowdry, Keniston, and Cabin (1970) have queried: " . . . are reported findings characteristic of *activists* of the left only, or are they characteristic of all individuals who privately hold left-wing political and social attitudes, including also those who are inactive? Are the findings characteristic of activists *of the left* only, or are they characteristic of all individuals who publically act in support of their convictions, wherever these may fall on the political spectrum . . . [p. 526; italics in original]?" In other words, it is at least conceivable that the inferred qualities of the "student activists" are associated with their left ideology rather than with their activism. Or, it is just as likely that all activists—whether left, middle, or right in their political orientation—share the same personal and social traits as a function of their being activists, not left-wing activists.

As an illustration of this issue, let us examine a study by Trent and Craise (1967). These investigators compared responses among three groups on a multiscale research instrument called the Omnibus Personality Inventory or OPI (Heist and Yonge, 1968). The three groups were 130 Berkeley Free Speech Movement arrestees, a random sample of 92 Berkeley seniors (using data obtained by Heist, 1965), and a national sample of 1385 college students (using data that Trent and Craise obtained). Trent and Craise concluded: "From these comparisons, it becomes apparent that few college students in general can match the positive development of those personality characteristics that distinguish student activists from their college contemporaries [p. 39]." Since it was student *left* activists under study, the question arises as to whether these qualities are related to the students' activism or to their left ideology. Another question arises as to whether or not right activists might also possess these presumably superior personality qualities. The confounding of activism and ideology, by failing to include at least right activist controls, does not allow an answer to these questions.

As another example, Katz (1967) reported higher verbal Scholastic Aptitude Test scores for (presumably left) activists compared with (unspecified) nonactivists and concluded that left activists were intellectually pre-eminent. Again, left activists may indeed be more intellectually able than their nonactivist counterparts, as Katz concluded, but this still leaves open the question of how they compare with ideologically right and with middle-of-the-road activists.

That student right activists have been studied so infrequently, either in and of themselves (Westby and Braungart, 1967) or as compared with student left activists (Braungart, 1966; Dunlap, 1970; Haan, Smith, and Block, 1968; Kerpelman, 1969b; Westby and Braungart, 1966, 1970; Winborn and Jansen, 1967), may reflect the relative scarcity of right activists to study on the campuses where most of the activism research is undertaken. It may, on the other hand, reflect the comparative inattention of investigators to the less visible, and perhaps less "exciting," student right.

Lipset (1968), Kerpelman (1969b), Cowdry, Keniston, and Cabin (1970), and Block, Haan, and Smith (1968) all independently have proposed the separation of activism and ideology in investigations of student political activism. The last-mentioned authors have succinctly stated the issue this way:

> Although there has been a tendency to equate social involvement and political activism with liberal politics, we have been impressed by the existence of an active protest group with a conservative political philosophy. The continuing presence of such individuals requires that activism be defined independently of political ideology if we are to extricate the correlates of activism *per se* from those of liberalism *per se* [p. 208].

Without instituting appropriate comparative studies in which students with different political ideologies are sampled within the activism dimension, it is impossible to state with certainty just what the attributes of the "new left" are and how these distinguish them from "radical right" and "moderate middle" activists.

Nonactivist controls

A further problem with some of the student activism research lies in the failure of many investigators to compare their findings on activists with findings from appropriate control groups of nonactivist students. If such control groups are not included in research designs for comparison with student activists, it is difficult, if not impossible, to determine whether or not the characteristics ascribed to the activists are actually characteristics common to all college youth. Keniston's intensive interview study (1968) of a group of Vietnam Summer volunteers provides interesting insights into the backgrounds and motivations of a highly committed group of left activists. Yet, because of the absence of appropriate control groups, unanswered questions remain concerning the qualities that are unique to the students Keniston studied and those that are common to all college and university students.

Even if control group procedures are instituted, the controls must be appropriate if interpretation of the data obtained is to be meaningful. Frequently, control groups with whom left activist student groups are compared consist of randomly selected nonactivist students (cf. Flacks, 1967; Heist, 1965; Trent and Craise, 1967; Watts and Whittaker, 1966). Now within the omnibus category of students called "nonactivists" by most investigators may be politically nonactive students whose thinking is radically left and others whose ideological bent is highly conservative. It is obvious that if political ideology is not considered, then comparing left activists with nonactivists of unknown ideology is akin to comparing apples and bicycles. The resulting conclusions are tenuous at best.

Furthermore, randomly selected nonactivist controls are frequently not matched with activists for what, lacking a better term, could be called "participatory activity." Members of activist groups share at least one feature in common—they all participate in an organized group. A random selection of students as control subjects will include students who may or may not belong to an organized group. This may then result in misleading conclusions, for qualities thought to be associated with a tendency to engage in *political* activity may merely be qualities associated with a tendency to engage in *any* activity. The only way to tell which is the case would be to select politically nonactive control students from organizations (but from organizations which are not political in nature, of course). While perhaps trivial, this is a point that should at least be considered in investigations of student activists. None of the studies referred to above which used nonactivist controls selected those control students from extant, nonpolitical campus organizations.

Measurement and interpretation

Because many research investigations of student activism have been stimulated by momentary events (such as sit-ins and demonstrations), the measures of personality and intellectual traits used in these investigations frequently have borne the earmarks of being hastily chosen and inappropri- ately interpreted. It has also seemed to be the case that, owing to the practical difficulties involved in investigating so sensitive (both socially and legally) an area, indirect measures, rather than direct ones, have been taken of students' personality, intellectual, and value attributes. Finally, researchers have been prone to interpret personality measures loosely and to make unwarranted positive value judgments about personality traits. The result has been that whatever firm knowledge appears to have emerged from the activism research is, upon more careful examination, very shaky indeed.

Some examples might elucidate these assertions. As quoted above, Trent and Craise (1967) spoke of (left) activists' personality characteristics in very positive terms. Closer examination of the seven OPI scales upon which their conclusions were based reveals that most of the scales do not measure what would commonly be thought of as personality attributes. Three of the seven OPI scales (the Thinking Introversion, Complexity, and Estheticism Scales) pertain to intellectual orientation, two scales (the Autonomy and Religious Liberalism Scales) assess the respondents on liberalness and conservativeness, and only two scales (the Impulse Expression and the Lack of Anxiety Scales) are concerned with personality or ego functioning (Heist and Yonge, 1968). Of the latter two scales, the left activists scored higher in Impulse Expression and lower on Lack of Anxiety than the nonactivist students. An extremely high Impulse Expression score (the activists' mean score ap-proached being extremely high) can indicate "frequent feelings of rebellion and aggression [Heist and Yonge, 1968, p. 5]." A lower score on the Lack of Anxiety Scale indicates a higher anxiety level. It is thus difficult to see how, on the basis of these OPI Scale scores, it can be concluded that " . . . few college students in general can match the positive development of those personality characteristics that distin-guish student left activists from their college contemporaries [Trent and Craise, 1967, p. 39]." It is further interesting to note that these investigators' report of Heist's (1965) OPI data did not include scores on two other scales of ego functioning (the Social Alienation and Social Introversion Scales) reported by Heist. The left activists' scores on these scales would indicate that they were more withdrawn and isolated than their nonactivist counterparts.

Although Heist (1965) himself did not extrapolate from his data in the manner just described, others have. One writer cited these same data, among others, to support his assertions about " . . . the strength and richness of their [left activists'] intellectual, aesthetic, and emotional endowment [Katz, 1967, p. 16]." This conclusion, in my opinion, is unwarranted on the basis of the empirical data from which it is drawn. Indeed, there are recent studies which suggest, contrary to the earlier contentions of Katz (1967), Keniston (1967), Trent and Craise (1967), and Bay (1967), that left activists may be less adjusted, in certain respects, than their nonactivist nonleftist counterparts. Whittaker and Watts (1971) found, for example, that their left activist subjects (who were, incidentally, also from Berkeley) were more autonomous and sought change of routine more than did a cross section of Berkeley students. The former students also, however, had less self-control, were more emotionally labile, were more exhibitionistic, and were more aggressive than the latter students. The point of all this is not to assert that left activists do not possess certain desirable personality traits, nor to suggest that some personality traits are more desirable than others. The point is simply to suggest that conclusions about "positive" personality development need to be thought through more carefully than has been the case thus far with declarations about the personality of left activists. Statements of such certitude as those of Katz and of Trent and Craise simply do not seem to be warranted on the basis of current evidence.

Nowhere is the tendency to draw questionable conclusions,

based upon equally questionable measures, so pronounced as it is in the area of intellectual ability of student left activists. Some examples might illustrate this point. Somers (1965) referred to higher *self-reported* grade point averages of a sample of left activists at Berkeley as an indication of their greater intellectual ability. Bay (1967) and Katz (1967), in their reviews, both cited this in support of their assumptions concerning the superior intellectual ability of student left activists. Yet Watts and Whittaker (1966), examining *actual* records of grade point average, found no differences between left activists and nonactivist students at Berkeley. Even more pertinent is the finding that a sample of left activists at Yale viewed themselves as higher in class standing than did a sample of Yale nonactivists, even though substantive evidence of academic ability (College Entrance Examination Board scores, high school rank, and actual grade point average) revealed no differences between the two groups on these indices (Geller and Howard, 1969). This finding, along with that of Watts and Whittaker, seriously calls into question the accuracy of self-reported estimates of academic ability as a measure of intellectual endowment.

Heist (1965) reported significantly higher grade point averages, based upon registrar's data, of left activists as compared with randomly selected nonactivists, but without supporting numerical data given, it is difficult to evaluate fully this finding.[1] Katz (1968) also reported similar findings, and *with* supporting numerical data. But in another publication, Katz (1967) also cited Flacks (1967) to support his contention that left activists have higher grade point averages, and therefore higher intelligence, than nonactivists, even though the latter's data were based upon self-reports, and numerical data and tests of statistical significance were not reported in Flacks's published article. The statistical tests that I have carried out on the data collected by Flacks, kindly provided by him,[2] do indicate that "high" and "low" activists differed significantly in self-reported grade point average. But other data collected by Flacks at the same time which did not appear in his published article indicate that the same samples did not differ significantly in self-reported class standing. Two other groups of activists and nonactivists sampled by Flacks did not differ on self-reported grade point average, and yet another comparative sample of student left activists and student right activists that Flacks studied also did not differ to any great extent on self-reported grade point average. Finally, a national survey of student activists which examined institutional records of total grade point averages of juniors and seniors found that the direct relationship between grade point average and political activism held only in high quality institutions. The investigators even found that ". . . among the least selective colleges, there appears to be a slight *inverse* relationship between grades and activism [Kahn and Bowers, 1970, p. 45. Italics added]." It should be noted that, with rare exceptions, most of the studies of intellectual indices of left activists discussed here have been conducted at elite institutions. I have more to say about the implications of this below.

Grade point average is at best a very indirect measure of intelligence. Yet even more indirect measures have often been cited in support of the view that left activists are more intelligent than nonactivists. Heist's (1965) data on the Intellectual Disposition Categories of the Omnibus Personality Inventory have been cited frequently in support of contentions " . . . that many of these students are the most bright and able students to be found on the nation's campuses [Trent and Craise, 1967, p. 38];" "that the activists are recruited particularly from the intellectually able and interested students . . . [Katz, 1967, p. 14];" and that there is " . . . an apparent preponderance of intelligence and intellectual resources on the left side of the political spectrum . . . [Bay, 1967, p. 76]." Yet, the Intellectual Disposition Categories are simply indicative of "an intellectual-scholarly disposition [Heist and Yonge, 1968, p. 23]," not intelligence *per se*. "The absence of intrinsic intellectual interests does not correlate strongly with poor academic achievement . . . [Heist and Yonge, 1968, p. 25]." The six scales that comprise the categories correlate only slightly and on the whole nonsignificantly with measures of academic aptitude (Heist and Yonge, 1968; see especially their Tables 9, 10, and 16). In other words, students can score in the low direction on the Intellectual Disposition Categories of the OPI and still possess perfectly adequate intelligence. In the activism research literature, this widely used measure of intellectual disposition has too often been considered synonymous with intellectual ability. It definitely is not.

Few studies have attempted to measure the intelligence of activists directly. One reported a slightly higher mean verbal intelligence test score for a group of student left activists at Berkeley than for a group of randomly selected nonactivist Berkeley students (Watts, Lynch, and Whittaker, 1969). Statistical tests were not reported for these data, but my own analysis of the raw data, kindly provided by Dr. Whittaker (Personal communication, August 1969) revealed that the difference was not statistically significant. In other words, the slightly higher intelligence scores of the left activists could have occurred by chance. Another investigation, conducted at a large, nonelite, northeastern state university, reported a statistically significantly higher mean verbal intelligence test score for activist, as contrasted with nonactivist, university students. This difference, however, held for ideologically left, center, and right activists *combined* as contrasted with left, center, and right non-activists *combined.* Left activists alone did not score higher on this measure than did any other subgroup (Kerpelman, 1969b). These findings suggest that the oft-asserted intellectual superiority of left activists has little, if any, empirical support.

Criteria for selection

The issue of the critieria used for selection of activist students for study is obviously an important one. The student's identification of himself as belonging to an activist organization has been accepted generally as a selection criterion in research on activism. In only a few studies, however (Abramowitz, 1972; Geller and Howard, 1969; Kerpelman, 1969b; Loken, 1970), has an attempt been made, in addition, to obtain a quantitative index of extent of political activism. Even fewer studies (e.g., Abramowitz, 1972; Kerpelman, 1969b; Loken, 1970) have attempted to use a quantified index of political ideology as a selection criterion.

Furthermore, activist organizations contain a range of participants from the highly committed to the hangers-on. Again, only a few investigators have considered this variable. Sampson (1967) was one of the first to suggest its importance; Keniston (1968) and Winborn and Jansen (1967) studied student activist leaders, but, unfortunately, they made no comparisons between these highly committed leaders and their less committed organization members.

Most investigations that attempt to examine the properties of student activists must, by their very nature, reveal to the students that the reason for their being selected for study is because of their activism. Yet subjects' awareness that they are being studied as members or representatives of activist groups may affect the way they respond to questionnaires and other measuring instruments. It has been suggested that:

> ... when subjects are aware that they are being questioned as members or representatives of a particular group, they may attempt to present themselves in a manner which they view as consistent with the public image of that group. In keeping with this, the responses of student activists to attitude surveys and psychological tests may be influenced by the popularly known findings of social scientists as well as the familiar image created by the mass media [Geller and Howard, 1969, p. 15].

It is obviously very difficult to study student activists without their knowledge and cooperation. Only in Geller and Howard's (1969) investigation, by means of a nonreactive index of politically active commitment, were students investigated without being aware of the reasons for their selection. It is also difficult to study student activists anonymously, as names are usually required to keep the research data in order. Yet students may respond in a much different manner if they know that their names will be associated with their responses than if anonymity is assured them, or they even may be hesitant to respond at all, as Walsh (1969) has reported.

Another issue in the selection of students for study is that of the eliteness of the campuses on which most student activism research has been conducted, and the possibility that campus eliteness may have been confounded with the psychological "eliteness" so frequently attributed to student left activists. As is suggested by this review, and as Block, Haan, and Smith (1968) have indicated in a similar review, "The researches to date have been conducted largely on the elite university campuses of America where intellect, inquiry, and criticism are reinforced. Their findings . . . may not hold for other college environments [p. 213]." Indeed, one study on the demographic background variables of radical and conservative political activists, conducted on a "non-elite" university campus (Dunlap, 1970), failed to find the social background differences reported so often in other studies. Another study (Kahn and Bowers, 1970) found that apparent socioeconomic background differences between activists and nonactivists tended to disappear when institutional quality was taken into account.

The nature of the student activism phenomenon ideally calls for examination that extends beyond the boundaries of any one particular institution of higher education. Practical considerations frequently prohibit the investigation of student activism at more than one campus at a time. Since this usually means that different methodologies and measurements prevail in each investigation, comparability of results suffers. Most of the studies discussed so far have been separate studies of student sociopolitical activists on single campuses. Only a few of them (Braungart, 1966; Flacks, 1967; Haan, Smith, and Block, 1968) examined students from more than one campus simultaneously, and only Peterson's (1966, 1968b) mail surveys of the scope of organized student protest, Kahn and Bowers's (1970) recent investigation, and Astin's (1968) large-scale longitudinal study of college students have attempted to investigate differences related to institutions. While the sum total of separate researches at separate campuses may yield useful findings and provocative hypotheses, the diversity of methodologies and instruments used makes it difficult to obtain a more global picture of the student activism movement. It would seem, then, that a useful addition to the study of activism would be to sample campuses as well as students.

As I reviewed the research literature on student activism, one thing seemed clear—that our knowledge of the personal and environmental determinants of student activism was *not* clear. Too much of the previous research confused activism and ideology, failed to study appropriate control groups (or to investigate any control groups at all), misinterpreted the measuring instruments used, set loose criteria for the selection of subjects and lacked adequate quantification of those criteria, and did not allow comparisons of methods or findings from study to study or from campus to campus. Recognizing these shortcomings was the first step in attempting to overcome them. Building upon the experience of investigators before me, and with the benefit of the hindsight naturally unavailable to them, I attempted to design a study that would perhaps avoid some of the pitfalls in which earlier work had become snarled. The design of my investigation, and some of the bases for it, constitute what is discussed in the next chapter.

2 / A DESIGN FOR INVESTIGATION

For all of its limitations, the research literature reviewed in the previous chapter, if nothing else, has served to suggest some hypotheses concerning the student activism movement. Before going on to discuss the general outline of the investigation, I would like to discuss these hypotheses. While this research project did not align itself with one hypothesis or the other, it did attempt to shed light on these speculations by providing data germane to them.

Some Current Hypotheses

One thing that quickly becomes apparent from scrutinizing the student activism literature is that many investigators and observers seem to adopt a "with 'em" or "agin' 'em" attitude. The former manifests itself in what I would call the "extraordinary leftist" hypothesis. That position avers that student left activists come from remarkably positive and privileged backgrounds and, because of this, they can face life as psychologically rich, extraordinarily well-adjusted individuals. Their activism is a reaction to the ills that they see in the world around them, an activism made possible because the strength and richness of their personality and intellectual endowments allow them to face the rigors and abrasions that are part of movement activities. Among those who seem to share this view to a greater or lesser extent are Bay (1967),

Flacks (1967), Heist (1965), Katz (1967), Sampson (1967), and Trent and Craise (1967).

The opposite view is one that I would propose be called the "maladjusted leftist" hypothesis. That view postulates that the student left activists' propensity to engage in activities which are contrary to the norms of the larger society around them is an extension to that larger society of the hostility that they feel toward their parents. This hypothesis has been even less fortified by research efforts, so it remains more in the realm of speculation than its counterpart. Bettelheim (1969) and Feuer (1969) are two who have speculated in this direction. Whittaker and Watts (1971), while by no means embracing the "maladjusted leftist" hypothesis, did present evidence suggesting that student left activists possess, in addition to positive personality traits, negative ones as well.

Fewer scholarly observers have even seemed to care to conjecture about the personal motivations of right activists. Interestingly enough, of the postulations that have been made, none, that I know of, could be considered to be parallel to the "extraordinary leftist" hypothesis. Whatever else they have been called, right activists have not been called psychologically adjusted. Bay (1967) has ventured to postulate that anyone embracing a rightist philosophy is, prima facie, maladjusted, and Bay therefore could be considered a proponent of the "maladjusted rightist" hypothesis.

These psychological hypotheses have rough parallels in sociological analysis. The present research project did not address itself to sociological variables, but the sociological speculations deserve mention because, at least in the case of the "extraordinary leftist" hypothesis, they have served as a framework and provided a support for some of the psychological hypotheses. One such sociological conception is derived from the findings that indicate that student left activists come from family backgrounds that are permissive psychologically, upper middle class sociologically, and liberal politically. Student left activism in this view is seen as a positive extension of early socialization processes within the family, rather than a negative rebellion against the family. Keniston (1968), although not necessarily embracing it, has called this hypothesis the "red-diaper-baby" hypothesis, and in its general outlines, it is roughly analogous to the "extraordinary leftist" psychological thesis. On the other side of the coin, the "maladjusted leftist" hypothesis has its rough approximation in the "generational conflict" hypothesis. Most cogently expounded by Feuer (1969), this viewpoint proposes that student movements occur, under certain social conditions, as a playing out of the almost universal conflict between generations that has its roots in unconscious hatred of sons toward their fathers. Student left activism, then, is a generational rebellion against parental authority figures that is displaced to the outside society when the historical conditions are right, as they are now.

Although there are no sociological parallels to "extra-ordinary rightist" and "maladjusted rightist" conceptual-izations, Westby and Braungart (1970) have refined and applied Lenski's (1954) "status inconsistency" hypothesis to student activism on the right as well as on the left. They found that while left activists tended to come from families with low ethnic status (eastern and southern European nationality, Jewish or Catholic religion) and high socio-economic status (upper levels of education, occupation, and income), right activists tended to have family backgrounds of high ethnic status (northern European or "Old Yankee" national origin, Protestant religion) but low socioeconomic status. The status inconsistency in these two directions in large part explicates the tendency of students to gravitate to politically left or to politically right organizations, according to Westby and Braungart (1970).

As I have indicated, the study reported here was guided only indirectly by these hypotheses. Its nature was more normative than hypothesis-testing, that is, a priori hypotheses were not tested. Rather, several general questions were posed which provided the framework for the content and design of this study. An attempt was made, in other words, to gauge the "state of the campus" and the "state of the students" on these important issues. Questions such as the following guided this study: What are the comparative demographic, ability, personality, and value characteristics of American college students who engage in different levels of political activism? Specifically, is the politically active student a different sort of person from the politically nonactive student? What are the comparative demographic, ability, personality, and value characteristics of American college students who espouse different political ideologies? Specifically, how do the little-studied students on the right of the political spectrum compare with their more intensively studied counterparts on the left? And what is the middle-of-the-road student population like? Are left activists, in particular, unique in any way, or do the personal qualities ascribed to them characterize the involved generally or leftists generally? Finally, what do the demographic, ability, personality, and value characteristics of American college students suggest about institutions of higher education today, and what do these characteristics augur for the state of the student movement in the future?

An Overview of the Study

The discussion in the previous chapter of the problems involved in attempting to study the personal and environmental determinants of student activism has suggested certain pitfalls to avoid and certain guidelines to embrace in designing a research investigation to deal with the questions posed immediately above. While the investigation reported in this book necessarily shares some of the limitations of the previous research, an attempt was made to recognize and deal with as many of them as possible. This was done by separating activism and ideology; by investigating activist students embracing the left, right, or center of the political spectrum and also investigating politically nonactive students who similarly embraced the political left, right, or middle; by using, for the most part, reliable and valid measurement instruments to examine the students' personality and intellectual characteristics; by using rigorous criteria for the selection of students to be included in the study; and by sampling students at more than one institution of higher education. Only in this fashion, it was felt, could a reliable body of information be obtained that would yield a more accurate picture of the personality, attitude, and intellectual attributes associated with activist and nonactivist students across the political ideology spectrum.

To accomplish these aims and to answer meaningfully the research questions posed, 291 students at three different institutions of higher education in the eastern United States were administered a two-hour battery of personality, attitude, and intelligence measures. These measures were selected because they covered a broad range of psychological attributes, yet were feasible to administer within a reasonable time period. An additional criterion for the selection of instruments used was that they were, on the whole, supported by a substantial amount of previous research that indicated that they were reliable and valid measures. In addition to instruments measuring personality, attitude, and intelligence properties of the students, the survey battery also included measures that would yield quantitative indices of the criterion variables of activism and ideology that were used in the selection and classification of the students.

The students who participated in the research all belonged to extant campus organizations. Based on their organizational membership, the students were initially classified as politically active or politically nonactive. The level of their activism or nonactivism later was confirmed by use of the quantitative measure of the students' political activism. The activist students were then further divided, both on the basis of an external independent rating of the political character of the organizations of which they were members *and* by a quantitative questionnaire measure of the students' own political stances, into ideologically left, center, or right categories. The nonactivists who participated in this study

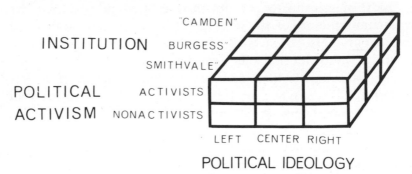

FIGURE 1. Schematic diagram of the research design.

were classified into the same three political ideology categories on the basis of the same measure of their political ideology. The resulting research design is indicated schematically in Figure 1. It may help the reader to keep this schematic design of the research in mind when the results of the investigation are discussed.

The advantage of a design for investigations such as this one is that it allows the delineation of those personality, attitude, and intelligence characteristics which are associated with activism *per se*, those which are correlated with ideology *per se*, and those which are associated with institution *per se*. A definite further advantage, moreover—and an important one—is that it allows a distinction to be made concerning which psychological qualities are associated with interactions of these three dimensions. It allows, for example, the determination of whether left activists possess certain unique characteristics, or whether right-wing politically nonactive students at a particular institution diverge in any particular manner from the other student subgroups. It is this type of differentiation, wherein the effects of ideology *and* activism *and* institution are examined in interaction, that has been notably absent from previous investigations and that was striven for in this one.

3 / THE INVESTIGATION

As we have seen, much of the research on student activism seems to have been done under less than ideal conditions. Stimulated by protest or confrontation, researchers have had to select measurements hastily in their attempts to discern the personal and social determinants of the students' protest activity, frequently with little time or opportunity to pay attention to control groups. Further, many of these research efforts were undertaken during the infancy of the still young activism movement, when techniques and conceptualizations may have been less refined. What I attempted to do in the investigation reported here—with the benefit of the hindsight and perspective that were unavailable to eariler investigators—was to make a more planned, more intensive examination of the personal and intellectual attributes and motivations of activist college students of all kinds, and of nonactivists as well.

As I have striven to emphasize, sampling, procedures, and instruments are important elements in research on student activism. In this chapter, the development of the research, the sampling, the instrument selection, and the measuring procedures are discussed in some detail. In this way, the reader who is so inclined can evaluate the strengths and limitations of the present study and, hopefully, use this study as a basis for further conceptual thinking and experimental refinement.

The Institutions

This research was conducted between November, 1968, and February, 1969. At that time, there was a high level of student activism on the American higher education scene. Students were protesting or demonstrating about ethnic studies programs, admissions and hiring policies, on-campus recruitment, and the Vietnam War, in addition to a variety of specifically local issues. The institutions selected for inclusion in this study were no exceptions, and they were chosen, in part, because of this.

Each of the institutions at which this research was conducted had to fulfill several other important criteria as well. First, each had to be an accredited, nationally known institution of higher education, not currently strongly affiliated with a religious body. What was desired here were institutions representing the mainstream of American higher education. The no-religious-affiliation proviso was instituted to avoid the possible confounding effects that affiliation of institutions might involve—to have measured the effects of religious affiliation would have expanded the scope of this investigation beyond practical bounds. Second, each institution had to be coeducational. This was for the purpose of obtaining as general a sample of students as was possible. Third, each institution had to be in the eastern United States. This criterion was included for the mundane reason of accessibility: since this project was not going to be a mail survey, institutions had to be chosen to permit me to administer the research instruments personally. Fourth, each institution had to have on campus political activists of the right, the left, and the center. This consideration was obviously for the sake of the research design. Fifth, each institution had to have on campus someone who would agree to serve as a liaison person between the administration, the students, and me. Although I did the actual administration of the research questionnaires, someone was needed on each campus who knew the institution well and through whom the myriad arrangements requisite to conducting the research on his campus could be made. Sixth, each institution had to grant administrative assent to undertake the research. Simple professional courtesy dictated this criterion. In addition, each of the institutions was selected to represent a different major type of institution of higher education, namely, a small private liberal arts college, a medium-sized private university, and a large public university.

As an initial step in the selection of the three institutions eventually to be included in this study, I contacted, in mid-1968, colleagues at various colleges and universities that fulfilled the first three institutional criteria discussed above. These persons were asked whether there were visible left, center, and right sociopolitical activist organizations on their respective campuses (center activist organizations were preliminarily assumed to be the campus student government bodies). If there were such groups on a campus (criterion four), the colleague was asked to suggest a possible liaison person, or consultant, on that campus. I then contacted the person suggested, explained to him the research project and his potential role in it, and asked if he would agree to serve in a paid liaison role for the research project. If he was agreeable to serving this consultant function (criterion five), he was asked to begin the necessary negotiations with the administration and with the campus organizations that would be asked to participate in the study (criterion six). It was emphasized to each consultant, and through him to the administration and to the student organizations, that I would

guarantee the anonymity of the institution, the organizations, and the individual students participating in the
research.

There were the expected unrewarding leads at first. One
campus was not a feasible one on which to conduct the study
because the students were too homogeneous, with the result
that politically left and right groups virtually did not exist.
One campus had left groups but no right ones, another, vice
versa. By the beginning of the 1968-1969 academic year,
though, arrangements were made to undertake the research at
three institutions of higher education which fulfilled all of
the criteria. Because of the promise of anonymity given to
them, these institutions are designated throughout this book
by code names. Comparative characteristics of the institutions are presented in Table 1.

Smithvale College

Smithvale College is a small liberal arts college enrolling just
over a thousand undergraduates. As can be seen in Table 1, it
is a highly selective institution, and a large proportion of the
faculty hold the doctorate. It draws its students from all over
the country, but mainly from the East coast. The campus is
fairly small and, although near a large city, it has a distinctly
quiet, unhurried atmosphere. Many of Smithvale's students
live on the campus, which impressed me, additionally, as
having an intimate but active atmosphere where most
students knew and interacted with one another. The
consultant at Smithvale was a psychologist associated with
the student counseling service. The research was conducted
there in the latter part of 1968. Shortly thereafter (and, I
assume, unrelated to this research effort), major campus

TABLE 1. Characteristics of the institutions.

Characteristic	Institution		
	Smithvale	Burgess	Camden
Size			
Male undergraduates	580	1,085	7,220
Female undergraduates	495	1,105	5,745
Total undergraduates	1,075	2,190	12,965
Graduate students	0	600	2,835
Selectivity			
No. applications, Class of 1972	2,214	3,200	18,158
No. accepted, Class of 1972	517	1,150	9,584
Mean SAT verbal score, Class of 1972	702	680	548
Mean SAT mathematical score, Class of 1972	692	680	572
Family income (dollars), Class of 1972	Unavailable	17,000	9,130
		(Mean)	(Median)

Living arrangements (percent)			
Undergraduates in dormitories	90	70	58
Undergraduates in fraternity or sorority houses	0	0	18
Undergraduates off campus	7	20	24
Undergraduates at home	3	10	0
Majors (percent)			
Business	0	0	8
Education	0	0	5
Engineering	8	0	8
Biological and Natural sciences	17	20	6
Humanities and Fine arts	38	30	17
Social sciences	37	50	12
Other	0	0	44[a]
Faculty			
Number	165	360	1,078
Percent holding doctorates	67	75	65

[a]Includes 24% freshmen and sophomores specifying only Arts and Sciences as a major.

demonstrations and counterdemonstrations over Black studies and other issues erupted.

Burgess University

Burgess University is a medium-sized private university enrolling over 2,000 undergraduates. As indicated in Table 1, it, too, is a selective institution with a large proportion of the faculty holding the doctorate. The undergraduate students are drawn from the entire country, with the largest group coming from New York and New England. Not as many undergraduates live on campus as at Smithvale. The atmosphere on the Burgess campus, which is also outside of a large city, is less rustic than that of Smithvale, and the Burgess students seem less close to each other than, but as active as (if not more so than) the students at Smithvale. The consultant at Burgess was an advanced undergraduate psychology major who was active in student affairs. The research was conducted at Burgess early in 1969. At that time, the campus was experiencing significant protest activity by many of the students over a wide range of issues.

University of Camden

The University of Camden is a large public university with an undergraduate student body numbering approximately 13,000. It draws its students largely from the state which it represents. Many of the faculty hold the doctorate. Like many state universities, it is not quite as select as the private institutions. Not as large a proportion of the Camden students live on campus as at the private institutions, and those students who reside on the Camden campus tend to

leave it on weekends to go to their homes elsewhere in the
state. The campus is typical of many state universities—large,
sprawling, and more impersonal because of its size, a
once-quiet state university on its way up in the academic
world. The quality of the faculty, as judged by the
proportion holding the doctorate, is high, and the quality of
the undergraduate students is only slightly below that of the
students at Smithvale and Burgess. Camden is not an "elite"
institution, but its faculty and students are of good quality.
The consultant at Camden was a graduate student in
psychology with some knowledge of undergraduate student
activities. The investigation was conducted at Camden late in
1968, during which time major demonstrations and counterdemonstrations revolving around on-campus recruiting were
occurring on the campus.[1]

The Organizations

The initial step in the selection of the campus organizations
which would be requested to participate in this study was to
obtain a preliminary prerating of the political character or
stance of the various groups. For this purpose, an Organizational Rating Sheet was compiled for each campus. On it
were listed the politically oriented organizations and a
sampling of the nonpolitical organizations on that particular
campus. Copies of this instrument were distributed to all of
the faculty members in the political science department at
each institution, asking them to rate, to the best of their
knowledge, the political character of the organizations listed.
It was recognized, and explained to them in the covering
letter accompanying the rating sheet, that political science
faculty were not necessarily experts on their institution's

student organizations, but that, just the same, their "educated guess" about them would be likely to be of some use. The covering letter and the form of the Organization Rating Sheet, from which all identifying information has been removed to preserve the anonymity of the institutions and organizations, are reproduced in Appendix A.

On the basis of the prerating returns,[2] summarized in Table 2, it seemed reasonable to presume that the left, middle, and right activist organizations chosen to participate in the research would be very likely to include members who were, indeed, left, middle, and right in political orientation. Politically nonactive target organizations were nonpolitical clubs that received preratings describing their ideology as moderate in relation to other nonactivist clubs. The word "target" is used to describe the organizations because the preratings of them were simply used as a preliminary basis to select organizations which would be likely to consist of left-, center-, or right-oriented students. Actual measurement of the students' political orientation was made during administration of the research instruments. This, not just the students' political organization membership, was the important index of the political ideology criterion variable.

The leaders of the target organizations were approached individually by the consultant for the purpose of discussing the possibility of their organization's cooperation in the research. He explained briefly the nature of the research project to them. If the leaders of the organizations felt that their members might cooperate in the research, the consultant then approached the members, either at a regular meeting of the organization or via mail. The consultant explained to the politically active students, in general terms, that the nature of the research was to assess, directly and accurately, the characteristics associated with college student activism along the entire range of the political spectrum. To the politically nonactive student organizations, the consultant indicatod that they were being asked to serve as control subjects for a research project. The consultant dispensed additional information carefully, and only if the students asked, so as not to contaminate unduly the research findings that were to be obtained subsequently. The consultant indicated to all the students that anonymity would be guaranteed, that about two hours of their time would be involved, and that they would be paid for their time at a specified hourly rate that was consistent with the prevailing rate for student workers at the particular institution. Finally, the consultant requested students' commitments to participate in the research and distributed, to those who had volunteered, appointment letters specifying the date, time, and place at which the research was to be conducted.

As with the institutions, the organizations that took part in this research are described here only in a general fashion in order to preserve their anonymity.

Left activist organizations

At all three campuses, the left activist organizations were a local affiliate of a national student left organization. In addition, at Smithvale, an independent local left sociopolitical action organization was included.

Middle activist organizations

At all three institutions, elected representatives of the campus student government organization were considered in the middle activist group. In addition, at Smithvale, an organization of students who had campaigned for a moderate-to-liberal candidate for governmental office, and at

TABLE 2. Political ideology preratings of target organizations by political science faculty at Smithvale College[a] and at the University of Camden.[b]

Organization	No. ratings per category[c]					Judgment basis		Mean pre-rating
	1	2	3	4	5	Good in-formation	Little in-formation	
Politically active organizations— Smithvale								
Organization SA[d]	6					6		1.00
Organization SB[d]	6					6		1.00
Organization SC[e]		6				5	1	2.00
Organization SD[e]		6				4	2	2.00
Organization SE[f]				5			5	4.00
Politically nonactive organizations— Smithvale								
Organization SF[g]		4	1			1	4	2.20
Organization SG[g]	1	2	2			2	3	2.20
Organization SH[g]		2	3			1	4	2.60
Organization SI[g]		1	4				5	2.80
Organization SJ			5				5	3.00
Organization SK		1	3	1		1	4	3.00
Organization SL			5	1		3	3	3.17
Organization SM			4	1			5	3.20

Politically active organizations—

Camden

Organization	1	2	3	4	5			Mean
Organization CA[d]	9		2			7	4	1.36
Organization CB	5	3	1			2	7	1.56
Organization CC		5	3			3	5	2.38
Organization CD	2	2	1	2		1	6	2.43
Organization CE	1	4	1		1	1	6	2.43
Organization CF[e]		4	3	1		4	4	2.63
Organization CG[e]		2	2	3	1	3	5	3.33
Organization CH[f]		1	1	6	1	4	5	3.73
Organization CI[f]			1	1	3	2	3	4.40

Politically nonactive organizations—

Camden

Organization	1	2	3	4	5			Mean
Organization CJ[g]		1	5				6	2.83
Organization CK		1	6				7	2.86
Organization CL		1	6			1	6	2.86
Organization CM[g]		1	8			1	8	2.89

[a]Six out of six faculty members responded.

[b]Eleven out of twenty faculty members responded.

[c]The rating scale range is from extremely politically liberal—1, to extremely politically conservative—5 (see Appendix A).

[d]Chosen as a left activist target organization on the basis of the preratings.

[e]Chosen as a middle activist target organization on the basis of the preratings.

[f]Chosen as a right activist target organization on the basis of the preratings.

[g]Chosen as a nonactivist target organization on the basis of the preratings.

Camden, a student judiciary body, were included as middle-of-the-road activist groups.

Right activist organizations

At Smithvale, the right activist group consisted of the campus conservative organization. At Burgess, it consisted of a loosely organized body that had tenuous connections with a national conservative organization, plus a campus right-of-center political club. The right activist group at Camden included a local campus organization formed to protest the activities of the campus left organizations, plus a campus right-of-center political club.

Nonactivist organizations

Members of clubs which were not political in nature, who, in addition, did not belong to any politically oriented organizations, were the subjects for the politically nonactivist subgroups in this research. Nonpolitical club members were chosen as nonactivists, rather than randomly selected students, in order to control for "organization-joining," or "participatory activity," between the activist and nonactivist subjects. From these nonpolitical clubs, students were assigned, on the basis of their responses to questionnaires administered to them during the research procedures, to nonactivist left, middle, and right ideology subgroups. At all three institutions, the nonactivist clubs consisted of interest and hobby clubs, campus service organizations, pre-professional clubs, and the like.

The Questionnaires

The students who volunteered to participate in this study would receive, when they appeared for their research appointment, a booklet containing several questionnaires and answer sheets. The questionnaires were chosen to measure as broad a range as possible of personality, value, and intellectual qualities. Each of the questionnaires was selected because it fulfilled certain criteria, namely, objectivity, reasonable evidence for its validity and reliability, group-administrability, and brevity. Two of the questionnaires were specifically designed to yield a quantitative index of the criterion variables of political ideology and political activity.

Since the questionnaire package was the main source of data upon which the findings of this investigation were based, it is worth examining each questionnaire in some detail. Each is discussed here in the order in which it appeared in the research booklet. Data-gathering instruments which are not commercially available are, in addition, reproduced in Appendix A. That appendix also contains a discussion of the evidence of reliability and validity of each measuring instrument.

Code Number Instructions (CNI)

The CNI is a brief instrument designed for this project for the purpose of enabling each student to assign to himself a unique identification number that he would then place on all the questionnaire material that he subsequently completed. In addition to providing a unique identification number, the 15-digit code provided descriptive demographic information, such as age and sex, which is used subsequently to describe the student samples. The code number provided a means of keeping an accurate record of all answer sheets while still completely preserving each student's anonymity. Since names were not requested anywhere in the questionnaire booklet, there is no way of identifying any individual with any of the questionnaire responses. The CNI is reproduced in Appendix A.

Control Test AA (CTAA)

The CTAA was devised for research use with college student populations by the Institutional Research Program for Higher Education of the Educational Testing Service (Peterson, 1965). It is a 30-item group measure of college level academic aptitude which includes quantitative, as well as purely verbal, items. In particular, the CTAA contains 9 antonym items, 12 quantitative comparisons, and 9 verbal analogies. It has a 12-minute time limit and a possible range of scores from 0 to 30.

Survey of Interpersonal Values (SIV)

Devised by Gordon (1960), the Survey of Interpersonal Values provides indices of six basic motivational patterns, or values, important in a person's relationships with others in everyday life. The SIV consists of 30 sets of three statements, each set in a forced-choice format. The respondent must indicate for each set which statement of the three is most important to him and which is least important to him. The six values which the SIV measures are as follows:

Support (S): Being treated by others with understanding, encouragement, kindness, and consideration.

Conformity (C): Doing what is socially correct and accepted, and following rules and regulations.

Recognition (R): Being looked up to, admired, paid attention to, and being considered important.

Independence (I): Being free to make one's own decisions and to do things in one's own way, and having the right to engage in whatever action one wants to.

Benevolence (B): Doing things for and sharing things with other people, and helping others less fortunate than oneself.

Leadership (L): Being in charge of other people, and having authority, leadership, or power.

The possible score ranges are: S Scale, 1-30; C Scale, 1-39; R Scale, 1-25; I Scale, 1-32; B Scale, 1-30; and L Scale, 1-32, with the higher score indicating a greater amount of the characteristic named by the scale.

Gordon Personal Profile (GPP)

The Gordon Personal Profile is a widely used instrument that is purported to measure "four aspects of personality which are significant in the daily functioning of the normal person [Gordon, 1963a, p. 3]." It consists of 18 sets, or tetrads, of four descriptive phrases each. Each of the four personality traits measured by the scale is represented in each tetrad. Of the four statements in each set, two are of similar high preference value (that is, they are considered to be equally complimentary), and two are of similar low average preference value (that is, equally uncomplimentary). The respondent's task is to select, from within each item set, a phrase which is most like him and to select another phrase which is least like him. Through this forced-choice technique, the respondent thus makes a three-level ranking within each set of four items, and he does so in a way that controls for social desirability to some extent (Gordon, 1963a).

The four personality characteristics which the GPP measures are:

> Ascendency (A): High scores on this scale indicate being self-assured, assertive, and active in groups. Low scores indicate lack of self-confidence and passivity in groups.
> Responsibility (R): High scores on this scale indicate perseverance, determination, and reliability in doing a job. Low scores indicate flightiness, irresponsibility, and an inability to stick to a task which has little interest.
> Emotional Stability (E): As the name of this scale suggests, high scores on it indicate emotional stability and relative freedom from anxiety. Low scores are associated with anxiety, ego defensiveness, and low frustration tolerance.
> Sociability (S): Gregariousness and liking to be with people are correlated with high scores on this scale. Social introversion and restriction of social contacts are associated with low scores.

The maximum possible score on each scale is 36.

Politico-Economic Conservatism Scale (PEC)

Levinson's (1959) Politico-Economic Conservatism Scale, a revision of an earlier scale (Adorno, Frenkel-Brunswik, Levinson, and Sanford, 1950), served as the basis for the instrument that was used to measure the students' political ideology, one of the two criterion variables of this study. On the basis of this measure, the students in this investigation were screened and assigned to the appropriate political ideology subgroups. The twelve PEC Scale statements are concerned with political and economic ideological positions. The respondent indicates agreement or disagreement with each statement on a scale ranging from − 3 (strongly disagree) to +3 (strongly agree), with the zero point eliminated to force a preference. In scoring, each item rating is converted to a score ranging from 1 to 7 (where 4 is the neutral point), the items summed, and the total divided by 12 to convert the scores back to a 1 to 7 range. Low scores indicate political liberalism and high scores indicate politico-economic conservatism.

The PEC Scale used in this study (reproduced in Appendix A) was a modification of Levinson's scale.[3] Over the course of two previous studies (Kerpelman, 1968, 1969b), I modified slightly the wording of four items (numbers 6, 7, 8, and 10) to make the PEC Scale more current and to equate within the total scale the number of items worded in a "conservative" direction with the number worded in a "liberal" direction. The latter was done in an attempt to counteract the effects of acquiescence set (the tendency of some persons automatically to agree with questionnaire items).

Activity Scale (ACT)

The Activity Scale served to give a quantitative measure of the second criterion variable, political activism. Devised by Michael Weiner and me, this scale assesses students' actual and desired participation in activities revolving around political and social issues of a larger (as opposed to a purely local) nature. It does so by asking students to check, on a five-point scale, the extent of their activism in terms of physical participation, communication activities, and information-gathering related to political and social issues. The scale is reproduced in Appendix A.

The Activity Scale is divided into two separate subscales. The first 12 items, the Activity-Actual (ACT-A) Subscale, question the student on the average extent of his actual activity in the areas enumerated, i.e., his actual frequency of participation in various sociopolitical activities during the prior three years. The remaining 12 items, the Activity-Desired (ACT-D) subscale, ask the respondent to indicate the frequency of his activity, i.e., his desired frequency of participation in the same activities during the same period had he been free of all obligations. The score for each 12-item subscale consists of the sum of the individual item scores. Since the items are scaled on a five-point scale, the ACT-A and ACT-D scores could therefore range from 12 (low activity) to 60 (high activity). In this study, ACT-A scores served as a quantitative double-check on the political activism-political nonactivism criterion.

Quick Word Test (QWT)

The Quick Word Test, Form Am, level 2, was the second measure of intellectual ability administered to the students. Devised by Borgatta and Corsini (1964), it is a rapid group test of verbal ability. The test is composed of 100 items, each of which lists a word and then gives four alternative words, one of which means the same as the stem word. The respondent's task is to select from among the alternatives the one word that most closely corresponds in meaning to the stem word in that item. Scores could range from 25 (random guessing) to 100 (perfect score).

Guilford-Zimmerman Temperament Survey (GZTS)

In an attempt to obtain "back-up" information on some of the personality variables measured by the scales already discussed, I included five subscales of the Guilford-Zimmerman Temperament Survey (Guilford and Zimmerman, 1949) in the research battery. The GZTS is an instrument which purports to measure 10 factor-analytically derived aspects of personality in respondents of high school, college, and older age. The GZTS consists of 300 affirmative statements which are potentially descriptive of the respondent. The respondent answers each statment with a "Yes" if it is true of him, a "No" if it is more false than true of him, and a "?" if he cannot decide between "Yes" and "No." The five subscales (of 30 items each) chosen for use in this research were Restraint-Impulsiveness (R), Ascendance-Submissiveness (A), Social Interest-Shyness (S), Emotional Stability-Emotional Instability (E), and Objectivity-Subjectivity (O). The possible range of scores for each subscale is 0-30, high scores being indicative of the first-named trait and low scores being indicative of the last-named trait of each subscale.

Campus Activities List (CAL)

The CAL, reproduced in Appendix A, simply asks the student to list all campus organizations to which he belongs. It was used both to obtain a measure of the number of extracurricular activities in which the members of the various groups engaged, and to eliminate from the data analysis any supposedly politically nonactive students who belonged also to a politically active organization or organizations.

The Survey

In preparation for the research sessions, the consultant on each campus had arranged evening group appointments with the students who volunteered to participate in the research. Left activist, middle activist, right activist, and nonactivist student organizations were generally scheduled for separate two-hour evening time periods. I traveled to each campus in order to administer the questionnaire survey.

The students were instructed to take separate desks as they came into the room. At each desk were two pencils and a booklet containing the questionnaires. I introduced myself and then gave the following introduction and instructions:

> I am conducting research on various campuses on some of the concomitants of student political activity [In the case of nonactivist groups, the following phrase was added: "for which you are one of the control groups"]. I want to thank you for having agreed to participate in this research. A more tangible acknowledgment, in the form of money, awaits you upon the completion of your participation this evening.
>
> The general purpose of this research is to attempt to study the attitudes and interests of students of all shades of political persuasion [In the case of nonactivist groups, the phrase "students of all kinds" was substituted for "students of all shades of political persuasion"]. As such, I am not interested in identifying particular individuals with particular responses. In order to preserve your anonymity, yet to allow the proper recording of all the questionnaires, I am going to ask you, in a short while, to provide a code number, unique to you, which you will use on all your questionnaire answer sheets. You will not be asked to place your name on any of the questionnaire material.
>
> The detailed nature of the research can be communicated to your organization, if you wish, after the entire project is completed.

At that point, I instructed the students on how to supply their 15-digit code identification number. The first test in the booklet was the Control Test AA, which required oral instructions and timing. After that test was administered, the students then received instructions to complete the rest of the questionnaires, as per the printed directions in the booklet, at their own rate of speed. Printed instructions for completing each successive questionnaire appeared in the booklet before each instrument. Upon completion of all the questionnaires (which normally took 1½-2 hours) each student brought his booklet to me. His answer sheets were checked for missing responses, and he was then paid for his participation in the research project.

In all, 83 students comprised the preliminary subject pool at Smithvale College, 94 at Burgess University, and 114 at the University of Camden, for a total of 291 students. This initial student pool was then further screened to yield a total of 229 finally selected students. It was these 229 students who provided the data for the findings and conclusions of this study. The criterion screening of these students and further aspects of the methodology of this investigation are discussed in the next chapter. The reader who is not methodologically inclined may wish to skip (or, at most, to skim) the next chapter, for in it are the finer details of how the research data of this study were analyzed. The general outline of the investigation that already has been discussed should provide for that reader enough background information to understand the findings. For the reader who is interested in more specific technical details, the entire next chapter is replete with them.

4 / METHODOLOGICAL CONSIDERATIONS

After all the questionnaire data were collected from the members of the target organizations at all three institutions, preliminary screening was done by eliminating from consideration the data of those students who, while belonging to a nonactivist organization, indicated on their Campus Activities List that they also belonged to a politically oriented campus organization. The data of three such students, all from the University of Camden, were eliminated. The data of four students who filled out a fair portion of their questionnaires incompletely or incorrectly were also eliminated. These four consisted of two left activist students at Camden and one at Burgess, and one nonactivist student at Burgess. With this preliminary screening step done, the final step was to create "pure" ideology categories from the remaining activist student pool.

Criterion Screening

Although activist students belonged to organizations that were identifiable as left, center, and right in political orientation, they may have joined these organizations for a variety of motivations, both ideological and nonideological. This may have resulted, in some cases, in students belonging to an organization the predominant ideology of which was inconsistent with their own ideology as genuinely personally embraced. Some not-so-hypothetical examples may illustrate this point. On a campus where left-oriented groups hold sway, a conservative student may not wish to identify himself with a campus conservative group. He may, instead, aspire to election to the middle-of-the-road student government body. In that way, he may hope to avoid the personal opprobrium connected with belonging to an out-group while still hoping to influence campus issues in a conservative direction. Another, albeit trivial, example sees a politically moderate student joining a left activist organization because his friends have done so. These inconsistencies—between personal ideology and public ideology—are important, deserve investigation in their own right, and, indeed, have been studied with interesting results (see Cowdry, Keniston, and Cabin, 1970). In light, however, of the numerous statements made in the literature about the personal attributes of supposedly ideologically "pure" left- and right-oriented students, it was decided that, for this study, the findings would be most revealing if they were limited to those students whose personal ideology was consistent with their public ideological commitment. Hence, a student's public ideological orientation, as indicated by his membership in a campus left, center, or right organization, was a necessary but not a sufficient condition for his inclusion in the appropriate category in the research design. The additional criterion of having a personal ideological orientation, as measured by the Politico-Economic Conservatism Scale, consistent with his public orientation had to be met as well. Thus, students who belonged to a prerated left activist organization but who scored in the center or right range of the PEC Scale were dropped from further consideration, as were similarly inconsistent students who belonged to the middle and right activist organizations. Politically *nonactive* students were assigned to their left, middle, and right ideology subgroups on the basis of their PEC Scale scores solely.

The placement of students into left, center, and right ideology categories was accomplished by constructing frequency distributions of the PEC Scale scores of the participating students. Separate frequency distributions for the students in the left, middle, and right activist target organizations at each institution, and one for all nonactivist students at each institution, were made. These distributions are summarized in Tables 3 and 4, respectively. From examination of these data, it was apparent that political ideology was distributed differently among the three institutions. Specifically, the students at Smithvale and Burgess were more left-leaning in their political ideology, overall, than were the students at Camden. This being the case, the use of the same PEC Scale raw score cutting points at all three institutions would have resulted in the inclusion in the research of almost no right-oriented students at the two former schools and of few left-oriented students at the latter institution. Consequently, percentile cutting points, rather than raw score cutting points, on the PEC Scale at each institution served as the basis for assigning students to political ideology subgroups.

In using this kind of procedure to select the students, the ranges of the PEC Scale percentiles used for selection of left, middle, and right students were chosen so as to result in the elimination at each institution of the fewest activist students. Of course when a criterion of nonoverlapping ideological distributions is used in addition to a criterion of organizational membership, this necessitates dropping of some students. I felt, however, that the statistical power lost by elimination of some students' data would be more than compensated for in conceptual refinement by having nonoverlapping, "pure" ideology subgroups.

The PEC percentile cutting points selected for the left

TABLE 3. Politico-Economic Conservatism Scale raw score data for activist organizations before criterion screening.

| Institution | Prerated ideology of organization | | | | | | | | | | | |
| | Left | | | | Middle | | | | Right | | | |
	M	SD	Range	N	M	SD	Range	N	M	SD	Range	N
Smithvale	1.71	0.52	1.00-2.83	23	2.37	0.85	1.25-4.67	20	4.79	1.00	3.83-6.00	7
Burgess	1.90	0.68	1.17-3.50	14	2.28	0.96	1.50-4.17	11	3.43	1.14	1.67-5.58	10
Camden	2.42	0.97	1.00-4.92	36	3.42	0.57	2.67-4.25	11	4.49	0.91	2.75-6.17	12

TABLE 4. Politico-Economic Conservatism Scale raw score data for nonactivist organizations before criterion screening.

Institution	M	SD	Range	N
Smithvale	3.11	1.01	1.25-5.00	33
Burgess	2.97	1.00	1.17-4.83	57
Camden	3.93	0.77	1.58-5.33	50

ideology subgroups were the 1st through 24th percentile; for the middle ideology subgroups, the 25th through 74th percentile; and for the right ideology subgroups, the 75th through 99th percentile. Use of this selection procedure guaranteed the inclusion in this investigation of only those students in left activist organizations who were on the left end of the politico-economic continuum of their institution, those students in middle activist organizations who were in the mid-range of the continuum, and those members of the right activist organizations who were on the right end of the politico-economic range on their campus. The selection percentile ranges and corresponding raw score data for the PEC Scale are presented in Table 5. The numbers of subjects given in that table are the final numbers of students included in each subgroup in this research, and unless otherwise noted, these are the numbers of subjects in each subgroup that obtain in all subsequent discussions. All findings presented subsequently are for these 229 finally selected students.

Statistical Considerations

Before the examination of the results can begin, the statistical operations upon which the inferences and conclusions about the data were based should be discussed. The basic design of this research was an analysis of variance design which allowed an examination of differences not only between ideologies, levels of activism, or institutions, but also of various interactions of these effects. In this research, the data of the continuous descriptive variables (such as age, and year in school), as well as of each of the questionnaire measures, which are all continuous, were analyzed separately by means of separate least-squares solution unequal frequency analyses of variance (Harvey, 1960). These analyses are summarized in Tables 22-29, Appendix B.

TABLE 5. Descriptive data for Politico-Economic Conservatism Scale after criterion screening.

							Ideology						
Institution	Activism	Left (lowest 25%)				Middle (middle 50%)				Right (highest 25%)			
		M	SD	Range	N	M	SD	Range	N	M	SD	Range	N
Smithvale	Activists	1.29	0.17	1.00-	12	2.42	0.49	1.70-	13	4.79	1.01	3.50	7
	Nonactivists	1.42	0.14	1.69	3	2.65	0.55	3.49	17	4.09	0.50	7.00	13
Burgess	Activists	1.42	0.14	1.00-	7	2.08	0.34	1.70-	5	4.37	0.72	3.50-	5
	Nonactivists	1.44	0.20	1.69	9	2.75	0.51	3.49	30	4.11	0.36	7.00	18
Camden	Activists	1.78	0.48	1.00-	22	3.34	0.53	2.60-	10	4.95	0.65	4.10-	8
	Nonactivists	2.00	0.59	2.59	2	3.51	0.35	4.09	27	4.66	0.32	7.00	21

Differences among any of the research subgroups in the main analyses of variance of the continuous variables were further analyzed by appropriate one-way analyses of variance and by Newman-Keuls analyses modified for unequal subclass frequencies (Winer, 1962). Where findings of differences between research subcells on a variable are indicated subsequently, they are based upon one of these appropriate tests for simple effects. The acceptable level of statistical significance for all statistical tests used throughout this book was the $p < .05$ level. Any group or subgroup differences that are indicated in the subsequent discussion of the results of this research, even though not specifically delineated as "significant" ones, are differences that are significant at the $p < .05$ level.

At this point in our discussion of the analysis of the results of this investigation, it may be worthwhile to comment upon the subsample sizes. Because of the forced "purity" of the ideology categories that inhered in the method of selecting subjects, there were fewer students in some of the cells than might be thought optimal. I do not think, however, that this vitiates the results of this study because the analysis of variance statistic used to analyze the data *combines across* cells for the main effect and for the two-way interactions. Only in the case of the three-way interaction would cell size necessarily cause some concern about generalizing from the results, and in the case of some simple effects it might suggest caution in interpretation. For all the main effects and two-way interactions, however, the subsample sizes should be no cause for reservation.

Preliminary to computing any of the analyses of variance, Cochran's tests for heterogeneity of variance (Eisenhart, Hastay, and Wallis, 1947, Chapter 15) were performed on the variances of all Institution $\times$ Activism $\times$ Ideology cells. The results of Cochran's tests, for all of the continuous measures, are reported in Table 6. These tests revealed that, of all the measures, the Number of Activities, the Control Test AA, the Responsibility Scale of the Gordon Personal Profile, plus the Recognition, Conformity, and Benevolence Scales of the Survey of Interpersonal Values, were found to manifest statistically significant departures from homogeneity of variance. Examination of the variances for these measures indicated that, in the case of the SIV R and B Scales and the GPP R Scale, the variance for the left nonactivists at Camden was very small (see Tables 14, 15, and 17, below). This was due, most likely, to the small number of students in that subgroup. In the case of the CTAA, the variance for the Smithvale left nonactivist subgroup was small (see Table 12, below), probably for the same reason. In the case of the SIV C Scale, the variance for the right activist cell at Smithvale was very large (see Table 14, below). Only in the case of the Number of Activities variable was there more than one subcell variance which deviated markedly from the rest (see Table 10, below).

In light of the fact that there was only one marked departure from the range of the other variances for each of the questionnaire measures for which heterogeneity was found, and in view of the demonstrations of the only minor effects of moderate heterogeneity of variance on the assumptions for parametric analyses of variance (Norton, cited in Lindquist, 1953, pp. 81-85), parametric analyses of variance were computed for the continuous descriptive measures and for all of the questionnaire measures. Only in the case of the descriptive variable of Number of Activities was a parametric analysis clearly inappropriate, and findings based upon that variable should be considered extremely tentative. To be statistically circumspect, however, the

TABLE 6. Cochran's tests for homogeneity of variance.

Measure	df	C
Demographic variables		
Age	1	0.292
Year in school	11	0.114
Year at institution	11	0.100
Number of activities	6	0.435**
Dependent variables		
ACT-A	4	0.189
ACT-D	2	0.136
QWT	1	0.154
CTAA	20	0.132*
SIV-S	7	0.127
SIV-C	6	0.201*
SIV-R	9	0.153*
SIV-I	9	0.129
SIV-B	7	0.213*
SIV-L	12	0.139
GPP-A	1	0.146
GPP-R	7	0.191*
GPP-E	11	0.082
GPP-S	12	0.093
GZTS-R	6	0.119
GZTS-A	1	0.129
GZTS-S	3	0.096
GZTS-E	21	0.090
GZTS-O	8	0.113

Note.—k = 18 in all cases.
*$p < .05$.
**$p < .01$.

analysis of variance results for the CTAA, the GPP R Scale, and the SIV R, C, and B Scales should be interpreted with some caution.

For the few noncontinuous variables (all of them variables describing the students), chi-squares might have been appropriate to calculate. This was not done, however, because the cell frequencies were such that too many low expected frequencies would have occurred in the chi-squares, violating the assumptions for that test. The noncontinuous descriptive data are simply presented and not statistically analyzed for differences among subgroups.

Multivariate Analysis

In addition to analyzing the measures separately by individual analyses of variance, the measures were also analyzed in combination using a multiple discriminant analysis (Veldman, 1967, pp. 268-279). All of the 17 measures unrelated to the criterion variables of activism and ideology were analyzed by this method. Since the students were selected on the basis of their ideology and their activism, to have included the Politico-Economic Conservatism Scale, the Activism-Actual Scale, and the Activism-Desired Scale in the multiple discriminant analysis would have added little information, as the groups would probably have been most differentiable on these three scales. For this reason, these scales were not entered into the multiple discriminant analysis. Because the main interest of this research was in the ideology and activism dimensions, rather than in the institutions, and in order to keep the multiple discriminant analysis from being too cumbersome, the student groups were combined across institutions for the purpose of the analysis. Thus the multiple discriminant analysis was computed for six activism-ideology groups along 17 dependent variables. Since the maximum number of "factors" necessary to represent group differences is the number of groups minus one, this analysis yielded five "factors." Of these five, two were statistically significant and accounted for most of the variance.

Let us now turn to the main findings of this research project, findings that I hope represent accurately the characteristics of a new generation of young Americans.

5 / THE STUDENTS:
DESCRIPTIVE CHARACTERISTICS

The students who participated in this research "described" themselves in several ways. They "described" themselves in terms of the sheer numbers who participated or who did not participate in sociopolitical activities and in terms of the sheer numbers who placed themselves along the political ideology continuum from the left, through the center, to the right. They "described" themselves in terms of demographic information that they supplied in constructing their unique code numbers. And they "described" themselves in terms of their responses to the numerous questionnaires given them. The first two descriptions are the subject of this chapter.

The Numbers Game

It is a somewhat shaky assumption to consider the original pool of students in each ideology category who participated in this study to be representative of the actual strengths of these ideologies on their campuses. To assume that, we would have to assume that students in all of the subgroups had an equal propensity to volunteer for the research, and that is very likely not to be the case. It still may be instructive to examine the distribution of the numbers of students, however, for what it suggests about the activism phenomenon. To facilitate that examination, Table 7 gives the distribution of activist subjects in the original subject

58

pool who volunteered for the research, as well as the distribution of nonactivists of different ideological persuasions who also participated.

TABLE 7. Numbers of students volunteering for the research project.

Institution	Activism	Ideology		
		Left	Middle	Right
Smithvale	Activists	23	20	7
	Nonactivists	3	17	13
Burgess	Activists	14	11	10
	Nonactivists	9	30	18
Camden	Activists	36	11	12
	Nonactivists	2	27	21

One thing is immediately clear from an examination of these distributions, and that is that proportionally more left-wing students are activists than are middle-of-the-road students or student rightists. If a student leans toward the left, he has a greater tendency to engage in organized political activity than have his nonleft colleagues. Conversely, a rightist student appears to have a greater tendency to avoid organized political activity. Indeed, the liaison person at each campus reported having to search more intensively for potential right activist target groups than for left activist groups. Cowdry, Keniston, and Cabin (1970) also found that "The more liberal or radical the student's perspective, the more likely he is to be involved in social and political activities of all kinds [p. 26]." In light of this, the tendency to confuse activism with left activism, as discussed in Chapter 1, is perhaps understandable. Given these apparent relative strengths of the groups, what do we make of them? It may be that the conservative philosophy eschews group political activism in favor of individual efforts. Or it may be that the conservative students at these institutions felt overwhelmed or frightened by their (generally accurately) perceived minority status on campus, and they thus had no wish to be publicly identified as a rightist by joining a right-oriented sociopolitical organization. That there were proportionally more ideologically right than left students at all three institutions who did not belong to a politically active organization (and who therefore did not publicly identify themselves as rightists) supports both these assumptions.[1] Concurrently, it is also reasonable to consider that the relative paucity of right activists may additionally be a function of the kinds and locations of the three institutions surveyed. Lipset and Altbach (1966) have suggested that a large number of students and campuses are involved in right-wing student activity. Braungart (1966) and Peterson (1968c) have suggested that this kind of activism may occur more frequently at church-related colleges and professionally oriented colleges. Since these were not the kinds of institutions studied in this research, right activists may have been underrepresented vis-à-vis the larger national higher education scene. Nevertheless, the kinds of institutions studied here are the kinds that tend to set the course for American higher education, and consequently, examination of their students has a distinct advantage.

So far as the left-oriented students are concerned, their greater apparent propensity to identify themselves with activist organizations may be due to several factors. Politically left oriented students may find more in contemporary United States society with which to be dissatisfied and about which to actively protest. Alternatively, left activism may simply be the "in" thing on some college campuses, and some students may join them more for conformity motivations than for other, more purely ideological, motivations. At this point, conjecture about motivations for joining or not joining activist organizations, based simply on numbers of students belonging or not belonging, is a hazardous procedure. As we shall see (Chapter 6), the questionnaire findings on social acceptance concern do not support the latter assumption. At this point, it seems wise to delay further speculation on what the relative strengths of numbers imply about personal motivations of the students until Chapter 6, when we can examine measures of these motivations and values.

The original pool of 291 students who completed the questionnaires was pared down to the final pool of 229 students by eliminating students in left, center, or right activist organizations whose own personal political ideology, as measured by their responses on the PEC Scale, was inconsistent with the predominant ideology of the organization to which they belonged. It may be interesting, at this point, to examine the pattern of the "inconsistents" in each activist grouping, that is, the numbers of those activist students whose data were eliminated from further consideration because their personal ideology was inconsistent with their public ideological commitment. By comparing the numbers of activist students in each ideology group in Table 3 (before screening on the ideology dimension) with the numbers in Table 5 (after ideology screening), some interesting patterns emerge. At all three institutions, almost half of the students in the left activist organizations were dropped because they were not on the left end of the ideology distribution. This suggests that a fair number of students join these organizations for other than ideological reasons, some of which were suggested at the beginning of Chapter 4 above. The overall percentage of left activist "inconsistents" in this study (44%) is higher than the percentage of left inconsistents found at Yale (33%) by Cowdry, Keniston, and Cabin (1970). Indeed, at the two more elite institutions (Smithvale and Burgess) which correspond more closely to Yale than does Camden, the proportion of "inconsistent" left activists was about half.

Similarly, except at Camden, almost half of the students in the middle activist organizations were dropped because of inconsistent ideology. Examination of their ideological stance indicates that most of these students were dropped because they were too far left for inclusion in the center group. Here two interpretations suggest themselves. One is that students with a politically left ideological orientation do not join the campus radical organizations because they do not favor their methods or because they deem them to be ineffective, and, instead, they attempt to work through the more moderate student government organizations.[2] A second interpretation, more sinister perhaps, is that there is an attempt to "infiltrate" student government organizations on the part of the student left. With no further data, either speculation is just that—speculation.

Finally, except at Smithvale, there were some "inconsistents" in the right organizations, although proportionally fewer than in the left category. This may be because the minority status of the student right organizations on all three campuses calls for a stronger commitment on the part of those who belong to them than is the case with the members of the student left organizations. Although this suggests why the number of right "consistents" is greater than the number of left "consistents," the motivations of the right "inconsistents" are open to conjecture.

A complementary analysis of the greater propensity of leftist students to engage in political activity has been postulated by Lipset (1971). He has stated that leftists:

... view politics as an appropriate and even necessary university activity.... the less leftist students are, the more likely they are to disagree with this view, the more prone they will be to feel that the university should be an apolitical "house of study." Liberals or leftists, therefore, are much more likely to be politically active than moderates or conservatives. A relatively strong conservative stance will not be reflected in membership or activity in a conservative political club. This means that on any given campus or in any country, the visible forms of student politics will suggest that the student population as a whole is more liberal or radical leftist than it actually is. Since conservative academic ideology fosters campus political passivity, one should not expect to find much conservative activity.

Presumably, it takes a lower threshold of political interest or concern to activate a liberal or leftist than a conservative. One would deduce, therefore, that the average conservative student activist should be more of an extremist within his ideological tendency than the average liberal. Hence a comparison of campus activists of different persuasions should find a greater share of extremists among the conservatives than among the liberals [Chapter 3].

If we were to substitute "consistents" for "extremists" in the above statement, the findings of the present research strongly support Lipset's analysis.

Demographic Information

The 15-digit identification code that the students placed on their questionnaire material not only allowed the research records to be kept in confidentiality, but also allowed descriptive demographic information about the students to be gathered. It is that information that is discussed in this section. From this point on, any differences between groups that are reported in the rest of this book are differences that have been found, using the statistical procedures outlined in Chapter 4, to be statistically significant. One of the items of information that each student supplied in composing his code number was an indication of whether he was a leader or a member only in his organization. These data for all the subsamples are summarized in Table 8. It should be noted, however, that this information for the left activists may be misleading, for the students in these groups at all three institutions claimed that they made no hierarchical designation of leaders and members in their organizations. Granting this spurious factor, it appears that, except at Burgess University, the distributions of leaders and members among the various organizations at each institution are not markedly dissimilar. Another descriptive variable, sex of the students, is summarized in Table 8 also. Particularly striking is the fact that while the sexes were more or less equally represented among left and center students, there were, overall, twice as many males as females among right-wing students. Even more notable was the fact that there were no females in the right activist groups at Smithvale and at Burgess, and only three (versus five males) on the remaining campus. Braungart's (1966) survey of student left and right activists also found proportionately fewer females in right activist groups than in left activist groups. Similarly, L. Eugene Thomas (Personal communication, September 1970) counted a ratio of about three males to every female at a recent (1970) national convention of a student right activist organization.

Students had their choice of indicating, in their code numbers, one of twelve major areas of study they were pursuing. These were combined into the five classifications presented in Table 9, which reveals that a preponderant number of students at each institution major in the arts, humanities, and social sciences. Smithvale and Burgess students, moreover, appear to go in for the "hard" sciences more than do Camden students. If we examine Table 9 group by group, rather than institution by institution, an interesting finding emerges. This is that the frequently asserted conclusion that student activists, and particularly student left activists, are overrepresented in the arts, humanities, and

TABLE 8. Descriptive data for organization membership and for sex.

Membership

Institution	Activism	Ideology					
		Left		Middle		Right	
		Number of leaders	Number of members	Number of leaders	Number of members	Number of leaders	Number of members
Smithvale	Activists	3	9	6	7	2	5
	Nonactivists	2	1	4	13	2	11
Burgess	Activists	7	0	2	3	2	3
	Nonactivists	2	7	14	16	5	13
Camden	Activists	11	11	1	9	2	6
	Nonactivists	0	2	9	18	7	14

Sex

Institution	Activism	Left		Middle		Right	
		Number of males	Number of females	Number of males	Number of females	Number of males	Number of females
Smithvale	Activists	6	6	7	6	7	0
	Nonactivists	3	0	11	6	11	2
Burgess	Activists	4	3	5	0	5	0
	Nonactivists	2	7	20	10	13	5
Camden	Activists	11	11	6	4	5	3
	Nonactivists	1	1	2	25	7	14

TABLE 9. Descriptive data for major.

Institution	Activism	Ideology	Major				
			Biological, natural, physical sciences (No.)	Business, engineering (No.)	Arts, humanities, social sciences (No.)	Education (No.)	Other (No.)
Smithvale	Activists	Left	0	1	11	0	0
		Middle	2	0	11	0	0
		Right	1	3	3	0	0
	Nonactivists	Left	1	0	2	0	0
		Middle	4	0	11	0	2
		Right	4	1	8	0	0
Burgess	Activists	Left	0	0	7	0	0
		Middle	0	0	5	0	0
		Right	2	0	3	0	0
	Nonactivists	Left	1	0	8	0	0
		Middle	9	0	20	0	1
		Right	9	1	8	0	0
Camden	Activists	Left	1	0	19	1	1
		Middle	0	1	9	0	0
		Right	0	2	5	1	1
	Nonactivists	Left	3	0	1	1	0
		Middle	3	1	13	6	4
		Right	7	2	6	5	0

social sciences (Braungart, 1966; Katz, 1967; Watts and Whittaker, 1966) appears to receive only moderate support here. In this study, where data were obtained from nonactivist control groups, it was the case that, while left activists were slightly overrepresented in arts, humanities, and social sciences, and right activists were somewhat underrepresented, all other students, as well, seemed to prefer these majors.

The variables of age, year in school, number of years spent at the particular institution, and total number of campus activities engaged in (the latter obtained from the Campus Activities List) are summarized in Table 10 (and the analyses of variance of these four continuous variables are summarized in Table 22, Appendix B). The nonactivists were found to be, overall, older than the activists; left-oriented students were older than middle- and right-oriented students; and students at Camden were, overall, older than those at the other two institutions.

The results for year in school (where freshman = 1 year, sophomore = 2, etc.) and for number of years actually spent at the institution are similar. In both cases, the students at Camden were at a higher year level and had been at their institution longer than those at Burgess or Smithvale.

The analysis of total number of campus activities engaged in by each subgroup indicated that the activists engaged in more campus activities than the nonactivists. Smithvale students engaged in more campus activities than those at Camden or Burgess. At Camden, center and right students engaged in more campus activities than did the left students at that campus.

Bringing together the preceding results, we can say of the samples that the nonactivists in this study were older, as were the students with a left political orientation (as Braungart, 1966, also found), as were the students at the public

TABLE 10. Descriptive data for demographic information.

Institution	Activism	Ideology					
		Left		Middle		Right	
		M	SD	M	SD	M	SD
		Age					
Smithvale	Activists	19.67	1.44	18.85	1.07	18.71	0.95
	Nonactivists	20.33	1.16	19.24	1.75	19.23	1.42
Burgess	Activists	19.14	0.90	19.80	1.48	19.20	1.30
	Nonactivists	19.78	1.20	20.00	1.23	20.06	1.11
Camden	Activists	20.91	2.25	20.30	1.16	19.88	0.84
	Nonactivists	22.50	3.54	20.33	0.92	20.48	1.72
		Year in school					
Smithvale	Activists	3.00	1.54	2.46	0.88	2.00	0.58
	Nonactivists	3.33	1.16	2.41	1.23	2.62	1.12
Burgess	Activists	2.29	0.95	2.80	1.30	2.20	1.30
	Nonactivists	2.56	0.73	2.83	1.12	3.06	0.87
Camden	Activists	3.27	1.20	3.20	1.03	3.00	0.54
	Nonactivists	4.00	1.41	3.26	0.71	3.19	1.03

Years at institution

Smithvale	Activists	2.50	1.45	2.39	0.96	1.86	0.38
	Nonactivists	3.33	1.16	2.35	1.22	2.46	1.05
Burgess	Activists	2.14	0.90	2.80	1.30	2.20	1.30
	Nonactivists	2.56	1.01	2.80	1.10	3.06	0.87
Camden	Activists	3.27	1.80	3.00	1.05	3.00	0.54
	Nonactivists	3.00	0.00	3.22	0.80	3.10	1.18

Number of activities

Smithvale	Activists	3.92	3.29	4.46	1.45	5.43	5.44
	Nonactivists	3.33	0.58	2.47	1.28	3.08	1.12
Burgess	Activists	3.71	2.14	2.80	1.10	2.60	1.14
	Nonactivists	2.22	0.97	3.20	1.58	2.50	1.04
Camden	Activists	1.96	1.21	4.00	1.70	2.00	1.07
	Nonactivists	1.00	0.00	2.93	1.44	3.05	1.77

university. Congruent with the latter finding, the students at the public university who participated in this study were also at a higher year level than those at the private institutions. Since the participants in this investigation were recruited from campus extracurricular organizations, this suggests that students who attend a less selective institution of higher education and who are, presumably, somewhat less intellectually gifted than their counterparts at private institutions (see Chapter 6 for evidence of this), may postpone engaging in campus extracurricular activities until later in their college careers when they have become firmly established in their studies.

Consistent with previous findings (Kerpelman, 1969b), the political activists tended to engage in a greater number of campus extracurricular activities of all kinds than the nonactivists. There was a tentative trend for the left-oriented students at the state university to engage in fewer extracurricular activities overall than their middle- or right-oriented fellow students. The same trend has been found at another state university as well (Kerpelman, 1969b). These findings suggest two conclusions. Left-oriented students at the large public universities may be more single-mindedly political; that is, if they join any campus organizations at all, they tend to join the campus political organizations. An alternative conclusion suggests the possibility that left-oriented students at large public universities may be repelled by the ordinary nonpolitical extracurricular activities available to them and may thus shun them.

Before leaving this discussion of the demographic characteristics of the research participants, it should be noted that almost all of them were white. Since information on race was not requested, it is difficult to determine how many participants were not white. It is my (necessarily rough) observation that fewer than fifteen participating students were of other races. This state of affairs apparently reflected the composition of the institutions' student bodies and the organizations' memberships. No effort was made to include black activist organizations in the study, as the black student activist movement, like the high school student activist movement, is a different enough kind of phenomenon to merit special attention in and of itself, attention that is beyond the scope of this study.

6 / THE STUDENTS:
PERSONALITY AND INTELLIGENCE
CHARACTERISTICS

Having some idea of what the students were like in a descriptive sense, we can approach the main set of issues which stimulated this research, namely, the personal and intellectual attributes of the students and similarities or differences of these personality and intelligence factors from group to group. The multiple answers germane to these issues lie in the questionnaire findings. The discussion of those findings in this chapter is organized around logical groupings of the measures rather than being presented questionnaire by questionnaire in the order that they were presented to the students. The logical groupings are those which, on an a priori, common sense basis, appear to describe facets of the same areas of functioning.

Comparative Characteristics of Activists and Nonactivists

Activism

The Activity Scale was administered to provide quantitative evidence bearing upon the assumption that members of activist political organizations were in fact more politically active than members of nonpolitical organizations. The descriptive data in Table 11 for the Activism-Actual Scale indicate that this assumption was correct. The students selected as political activists were significantly higher in political activism than the nonactivists, as measured by this scale. Significant institution and ideology effects were also found. The students at Burgess, as a whole, were more politically active than those at Camden and at Smithvale. Left-oriented students were more active than center students who, in turn, were more active than students on the right. Examination of Activism-Actual scores within each ideology group indicates that the activist students scored significantly higher than their nonactivist counterparts at each level of ideology.[1]

The Activism-Desired Scale is not a measure of the actual activism in which the student engaged, but is, rather, a more "projective" measure of the amount of activism in which the student would *like* to have engaged. Scores on the Activism-Desired Scale are summarized in Table 11 also. The activists, as compared with the nonactivists, not only actually engaged in more political activity, as indicated by their mean Activism-Actual responses, but also expressed the desire to have engaged in even more political activity, as indicated by their Activism-Desired responses. On the ideology dimension, the students' Activism-Desired scores, like their Activism-Actual scores, were also ordered left-middle-right. Left students scored higher on the Activism-Desired Scale than did middle ideology students, who in turn scored higher than the student rightists.

The data from the Activity Scale quantitatively support the qualitative expectation that members of politically active organizations would engage in more sociopolitical activity than would members of nonpolitical organizations.[2] Student activists also expressed a desire to engage in more political activity than the nonactivists, as might be expected. That left-oriented students were more active in social and political

TABLE 11. Descriptive data for activism measures.

Institution	Activism	Ideology					
		Left		Middle		Right	
		M	SD	M	SD	M	SD
		ACT-A[a]					
Smithvale	Activists	40.83	8.67	27.69	4.66	27.43	5.71
	Nonactivists	25.00	6.56	21.59	5.29	20.39	6.65
Burgess	Activists	46.14	6.44	36.40	6.69	32.00	13.21
	Nonactivists	27.44	5.55	25.57	8.29	20.72	5.02
Camden	Activists	44.23	8.45	33.20	7.41	24.25	4.43
	Nonactivists	29.00	9.90	20.04	4.82	20.24	5.06
		ACT-D[b]					
Smithvale	Activists	51.75	7.41	40.62	8.15	38.71	6.37
	Nonactivists	38.00	13.45	33.12	10.28	30.69	10.54
Burgess	Activists	52.57	4.50	50.40	2.07	43.00	12.63
	Nonactivists	38.78	7.05	35.27	9.82	28.11	9.28
Camden	Activists	51.50	7.02	49.70	4.60	37.75	6.34
	Nonactivists	47.00	8.49	30.82	9.80	30.05	8.77

[a]Preliminary normative data from 73 state university activist and nonactivist students (Kerpelman, 1969b) indicate a range of mean scores from 16.43 (right nonactivists) to 32.71 (left activists).
[b]Preliminary normative data from 73 state university activist and nonactivist students (Kerpelman, 1969b) indicate a range of mean scores from 24.07 (right nonactivists) to 48.71 (left activists).

concerns (and also desired to engage in more sociopolitical activities) than students of other ideologies is congruent with the findings from a similar study at a large northeastern public university (Kerpelman, 1969b). These consistent results, plus the fact that there were more left than right students in the original subsamples in the activist category than was the case in the nonactivist category in this investigation (see Table 3), reinforce the idea expounded in Chapter 5 that there is a greater tendency toward political activity among left ideologists than among right ideologists. The hypotheses suggested by "the numbers game" above— that, on the one hand, student leftists may be more dissatisfied with American society and therefore more inclined toward political activity, and that, on the other hand, student rightists may eschew group political efforts or may be reluctant to identify themselves as rightists—are further supported by the measures of activism.

The differences among the institutions in overall level of political activity of students (where Burgess students were, on the whole, more active than those at the other two institutions) illustrate the finding of Astin and Bayer (1971) that nationwide there is a greater tendency for students at private universities to engage in sociopolitical protests than for students at any other type of institution. Another interesting interinstitutional finding emerged from the Activity Scale results. Comparison of Activity Scale scores of students at all three institutions investigated in this research with those I investigated earlier (Kerpelman, 1969b) reveals that mean Activity Scale scores were higher at all three of the institutions currently under consideration. This may be merely a relatively minor institutional difference. On the other hand, it may indicate that the level of sociopolitical activism on American campuses has increased gradually over time, as has been suggested by Peterson (1968b).

Intellectual ability

Two measures of intellectual ability were given to the students: the Quick Word Test, a measure of verbal intelligence, and the Control Test AA, a measure of academic ability. The results of both scales (see Table 12) are consistent and easily summarized: There were no significant differences along the activism dimension or along the ideology dimension, nor were there any significant activism-ideology subgroup differences. The only difference in intelligence occurred among institutions, wherein students at Smithvale College were revealed to be more intelligent than students at Burgess University, who in turn were more intelligent than students at the University of Camden, as measured by both of the intelligence scales.

The only significant differences in measured intellectual ability, then, occurred among students from different institutions. In light of what one might be led to expect from an uncritical reading of previous research on the intelligence issue (Bay, 1967; Katz, 1967; Somers, 1965; Trent and Craise, 1967), the present findings on intelligence are perhaps the most striking of all.[3] The failure in the present research to find differences between the two activism groups, among the three ideology groups, or among any of the six activism-ideology subgroups, in two direct measures of intelligence suggests that previously used indirect indices of intelligence (such as reported grade point average and scores on intellectual disposition questionnaires) are probably misleading, inadequate indices of intellectual ability. At best, those indices are negligibly correlated with intelligence. As Geller and Howard (1969) have shown, student left activists tend to perceive themselves as ranking higher in class standing than they are in reality, indicating that the self-report measures of academic achievement used in previous studies

TABLE 12. Descriptive data for intellectual ability measures.

Institution	Activism	Ideology					
		Left		Middle		Right	
		M	SD	M	SD	M	SD
		QWT[a]					
Smithvale	Activists	74.83	8.67	71.92	12.32	65.43	11.79
	Nonactivists	75.67	12.90	81.06	11.12	77.00	12.70
Burgess	Activists	73.71	12.95	68.40	13.07	61.60	10.74
	Nonactivists	65.56	10.44	65.27	13.36	65.28	14.72
Camden	Activists	59.73	14.66	64.10	13.31	61.63	20.16
	Nonactivists	65.50	23.34	56.96	13.67	58.33	15.41
		CTAA[b]					
Smithvale	Activists	27.58	2.43	27.39	1.61	26.14	2.55
	Nonactivists	26.33	0.58	27.29	1.90	27.77	1.30
Burgess	Activists	24.71	2.93	26.00	0.71	26.00	2.55
	Nonactivists	25.44	1.88	24.63	3.03	25.11	2.76
Camden	Activists	21.23	2.72	23.30	2.31	24.25	3.24
	Nonactivists	25.00	1.41	21.82	3.59	23.33	3.80

[a]Normative data from 5,792 college freshmen (Borgatta and Corsini, 1964) indicate percentile ranks as follows: 20 = 2nd percentile, 46 = 50th percentile, 81-85 = 99th percentile.
[b]Preliminary data from 663 college freshmen at three liberal arts colleges (Peterson, 1968a) indicate mean scores of 14.67, 19.44, and 20.86 at each of the institutions.

may well have been invalid. And as Heist and Yonge (1968) have indicated about their frequently used measure of intellectual disposition, it is negligibly correlated with academic achievement. These facts seem to argue that it is inappropriate to generalize from indirect measures of intellectual ability to intelligence itself, as has been done so frequently by researchers in this area. Certainly the evidence gathered in this investigation contradicts previous statements regarding the intelligence of left activists and indicates that a higher level of intelligence is not the exclusive province of any particular ideology or activism subgroup among college students.

Emotional stability

While several of the scales administered to the research participants measured various specific aspects of personality related to emotional adjustment, two scales yielded general indices of this property. Results of the Gordon Personal Profile Emotional Stability Scale and of the Guilford-Zimmerman Temperament Survey Emotional Stability-Emotional Instability Scale are presented in Table 13.[4] There were no significant differences among any of the groups or along any of the dimensions on either measure of emotional stability.

As measured by two scales of general emotional adjustment, then, no differences emerged among any of the groups on this property. Of course, it is always possible that the two scales were not fine enough to differentiate among any of the groups, but the fact that other subscales of the same questionnaires did indicate finer personality differences among ideology, activism, and institution categories makes that conjecture unlikely. Furthermore, the failure to find

TABLE 13. Descriptive data for emotional stability measures.

Institution	Activism	Ideology								
		Left			Middle			Right		
		M	SD	N	M	SD	N	M	SD	N
		GPP-E[a]								
Smithvale	Activists	21.92	7.01	12	21.00	5.94	13	25.00	5.72	7
	Nonactivists	25.67	3.22	3	19.71	5.29	17	22.54	5.49	13
Burgess	Activists	24.71	3.04	7	23.20	6.50	5	16.60	5.27	5
	Nonactivists	18.78	5.29	9	22.97	5.17	30	22.22	6.29	18
Camden	Activists	22.64	5.97	22	23.00	5.08	10	20.75	10.36	8
	Nonactivists	18.50	0.71	2	21.62	6.47	26	23.62	6.34	21
		GZTS-E[b]								
Smithvale	Activists	16.30	5.23	10	16.00	7.04	11	19.71	6.68	7
	Nonactivists	10.67	6.43	3	14.88	5.45	17	15.36	6.44	11
Burgess	Activists	16.83	6.88	6	13.20	3.83	5	13.00	7.04	5
	Nonactivists	10.50	4.57	8	16.79	4.92	28	16.29	3.98	17
Camden	Activists	16.12	5.40	17	15.50	6.04	10	14.88	6.38	8
	Nonactivists	16.00	0.00	1	14.32	7.33	22	16.80	5.63	20

[a]Normative data from 4,518 male and 1,329 female college students (Gordon, 1963a) indicate percentile ranks as follows: 8 (males), 7 (females) = 1st percentile; 25 (males), 23 (females) = 52nd percentile; 35 (males), 34 (females) = 99th percentile.
[b]Normative data from 912 college students (Guilford and Zimmerman, 1949) indicate a mean score of 16.3 and a standard deviation of 6.02.

differences in overall level of emotional stability in this research replicates similar findings in previous research. In one study (Kerpelman, 1969b), Gordon Personal Profile Emotional Stability scores were in approximately the same range as in the present research, and there were no group differences. In another study (Whittaker and Watts, 1968), no differences in overall personal adjustment were found between left activists and a random sample of students, thus supporting the findings of this research on a sample that is at least partly comparable. The evidence therefore suggests that there are no differences in an overall, general personality attribute called "emotional stability" or "emotional adjustment" among student activists and nonactivists of left, middle, and right political ideology.

The notion that left activists approach being "psychological noblemen," as characterized by Bay (1967) and by Katz (1967), and the opposite notion, expressed by less sympathetic sources, that left activists are maladjusted (Bettelheim, 1969) or are playing out authority conflicts (Feuer, 1969) both illustrate the pitfalls of speculation with little or no direct data behind it. Similarly, conjecture that rightists are prima facie maladjusted (Bay, 1967)—I have come across no serious scientific writing which suggests that rightists are "superadjusted"—also seems to be grossly overdrawn. All these views are quite probably exaggerations and oversimplifications—the picture appears to be more complex than they would suggest. It is appropriate, then, to turn to specific personality qualities that may more finely characterize the groups.

Social acceptance

Under the rubric of social acceptance I have placed the measures that seem to be relevant to a person's concern about the way he appears to others and the value that he places on his relative acceptability to, and conformity to, others. The pertinent scales are all from the Survey of Interpersonal Values; they are the Recognition, Support, Conformity, and Independence Scales. Data for these four scales are summarized in Table 14.

The Recognition Scale results indicate that middle-of-the-road students value recognition more than do right-wing students, who in turn value it more than do left-oriented students. While there were no significant differences on the Recognition Scale at Smithvale and at Burgess, the nonactivists at Camden were significantly higher on this measure than were the Camden activists.

The Support Scale results showed that the nonactivist students, overall, valued being supported and nurtured by others more than did the activist students.

On the measure of conformity, it appears that the students at Camden and Smithvale did not differ from each other to a significant extent in terms of valuing conformity, but that both groups placed a higher value on it than did Burgess students. Right-wing students valued conformity more than did either moderate or left students. At Smithvale, the rightists were higher in conformity than the other two groups; at Camden, both the rightists and the moderates were higher on this trait than the leftists; while at Burgess, there were no differences on this attribute among any of the ideology groups (perhaps because the scores of all of the subgroups there were already so low—a "cellar" effect). The interaction of Institution X Activism X Ideology on the conformity measure is illustrated in Figure 2.

On the Survey of Interpersonal Values Independence Scale, interestingly, the left and right students, overall, stood together, both indicating that they valued personal independence significantly more than did the center students.

TABLE 14. Descriptive data for social acceptance measures.

Institution	Activism	Ideology					
		Left		Middle		Right	
		M	SD	M	SD	M	SD
		SIV-R[a]					
Smithvale	Activists	8.67	2.67	11.69	4.80	9.29	3.04
	Nonactivists	8.33	2.89	12.29	5.00	11.08	2.72
Burgess	Activists	9.71	2.56	15.20	5.63	13.60	3.05
	Nonactivists	9.33	2.35	11.77	4.70	11.89	4.30
Camden	Activists	7.59	2.32	12.10	6.54	8.38	4.50
	Nonactivists	12.00	1.41	12.04	4.69	12.52	3.61
		SIV-S[b]					
Smithvale	Activists	18.67	4.56	17.39	5.88	14.29	5.85
	Nonactivists	14.33	6.66	19.65	4.74	18.54	5.45
Burgess	Activists	17.71	4.68	14.40	2.07	14.00	2.92
	Nonactivists	20.22	3.80	18.77	4.85	17.56	4.76
Camden	Activists	17.09	2.52	17.10	5.47	13.75	7.52
	Nonactivists	17.00	1.41	19.74	4.86	17.86	4.52

SIV-C[c]

Smithvale	Activists	5.00	1.54	5.39	3.20	13.86	7.69
	Nonactivists	6.00	6.08	4.88	2.55	6.00	4.22
Burgess	Activists	5.86	3.02	4.00	2.65	6.20	1.64
	Nonactivists	3.44	2.24	5.03	3.59	5.89	3.48
Camden	Activists	5.55	2.52	7.50	3.72	8.00	5.07
	Nonactivists	2.00	0.00	9.07	5.42	10.67	6.11

SIV-I[d]

Smithvale	Activists	22.25	4.31	22.77	4.05	20.86	7.86
	Nonactivists	22.33	8.62	23.00	4.36	26.00	4.55
Burgess	Activists	24.29	3.35	20.80	8.32	21.60	4.83
	Nonactivists	25.11	4.40	21.80	5.39	24.11	5.71
Camden	Activists	26.46	3.35	18.30	8.92	26.38	5.40
	Nonactivists	28.50	3.54	20.74	5.34	20.76	7.76

[a]Normative data from 1,075 male and 746 female college students (Gordon, 1960) indicate percentile ranks as follows: 2 (males and females) = 1st percentile; 13 (males and females) = 51st and 54th percentile, respectively; 25 (males and females) = 99th percentile.

[b]Normative data from 1,075 male and 746 female college students (Gordon, 1960) indicate percentile ranks as follows: 4 (males), 6 (females) = 1st percentile; 16 (males), 19 (females) = 55th and 53rd percentile, respectively; 28 (males), 29 (females) = 99th percentile.

[c]Normative data from 1,075 male and 746 female college students (Gordon, 1960) indicate percentile ranks as follows: 1 (males and females) = 1st percentile; 12 (males), 15 (females) = 50th and 51st percentile, respectively; 28 (males and females) = 99th percentile.

[d]Normative data from 1,075 male and 746 female college students (Gordon, 1960) indicate percentile ranks as follows: 3 (males), 4 (females) = 1st percentile; 20 (males), 16 (females) = 50th percentile; 32 (males and females) = 99th percentile.

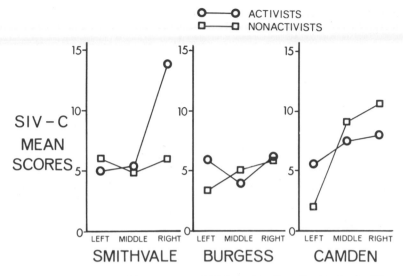

FIGURE 2. Survey of Interpersonal Values Conformity Scale, Institution × Activism × Ideology interaction.

The Institution × Activism × Ideology interaction on the independence measure is illustrated in Figure 3. Comparison of Figures 2 and 3 shows, with a few departures, generally opposite trends between conformity and independence across the subgroups; that is, the curves for these two traits are roughly mirror images of each other. Recognizing, of course, that scores for these opposing traits should be opposite to one another, examination of the graphs suggests that the two scales did indeed measure diametrical characteristics.

The various personality scales subsumed here under the rubric of social acceptance thus resulted in interesting, albeit complex, differences among the groups. To make these complex findings more intelligible, the discussion of them that follows ignores the less important institution differences that were found. From these measures, left-oriented students (activist and nonactivist alike) can be characterized as valuing conformity and recognition by others less, and valuing independence more. In not valuing conformity, they stand together with center-oriented students, whereas in valuing independence, they stand together with rightist students. That rightist students (again activists and nonactivists together) can value both conformity and independence highly appears at first glance to be a contradiction. Yet the conservative philosophy seems to call for an ability to tolerate such ambiguities, as exemplified by the glorification of individual enterprise together with a disdain for unusual or highly individualized behavior or appearance. I have more to say below, in the section entitled "Factors Differentiating Groups," about these apparently contradictory trends within the conservative students. Middle-of-the-road students appear, on the whole, to be less autonomous. They look for

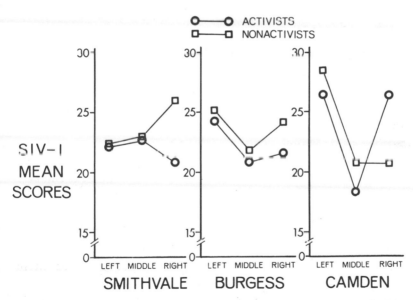

FIGURE 3. Survey of Interpersonal Values Independence Scale, Institution X Activism X Ideology interaction.

recognition from others more than do the rightists or the leftists, and they value personal independence least of all the ideology groups. They also, however, value conformity less than do rightists. The picture of the moderate students that seems to emerge from this is one of concern about social acceptance, but not at the price of excessive conformity.

Let us now turn from the ideology dimension to examine the results across the activism dimension. Politically active students as a whole (that is, left, middle, and right combined) value support from others less than do politically nonactive students. This seems logical, for to be a student activist, either in a student left or a student right organization, or in an elected student government body, almost invariably involves abrasive confrontations with others outside of the organization. If an individual requires understanding, encouragement, kindness, and consideration from other people, it is unlikely that he could remain comfortable being a member of a politically active organization for very long. This line of reasoning, supported by the data, runs counter to a more informal impressionistic line of thought that suggests that activist organizations function as substitute families. While more refined measures may eventually allow greater clarification of this point, for the moment we will have to adhere to the former, data-supported interpretation.

Social regard

Two subcategories comprise the overall rubric I have chosen to call social regard. The first, sociability or social interest, involves relations with other people that are expected to be reciprocal. A person's liking to be with others, to share social contacts—perhaps "gregariousness" is a good word—is what is included here. Concern for others in which reciprocity is not expected is involved in the second subcategory, social concern. A person's interest in helping others and in the well-being of others, without consideration of its direct return—perhaps "altruism" is a good word—is what is included here.

Sociability was tapped by two scales, the Gordon Personal Profile Sociability Scale and the Guilford-Zimmerman Social Interest-Shyness Scale. The results for these measures are summarized in Table 15. Of the two scales, only the Gordon Personal Profile Sociability Scale revealed any great differences among the research subgroups, wherein all the activists were significantly more sociable than all the nonactivists. Social concern, or "altruism," was measured by the Survey of Interpersonal Values Benevolence Scale. On that scale (the data of which are also reported in Table 15), the ideologically left students (activist and nonactivist alike) were revealed to hold this value more highly than did all the center students, who in turn valued benevolence toward others more than did the ideologically right students.

Although both the activists and the nonactivists alike belonged to organizations of one kind or another, there was a difference between them in terms of their sociability or gregariousness. It can be speculated that the activist students tend to join organizations, the purposes of which are to improve the functioning of their institution and the larger society around them, partially as an extension of their greater personal tendency to enjoy and value interaction with their peers. The finding on social concern is sliced in a different manner, yet it is perhaps more readily explicable. That left-wing students expressed more concern for others than did middle-of-the-road students, and that right-wing students expressed relatively little benevolent concern for others, might be expected. If this personality characteristic is present

TABLE 15. Descriptive data for social regard measures.

Institution	Activism	Ideology								
		Left			Middle			Right		
		M	SD	N	M	SD	N	M	SD	N
		GPP-S[a]								
Smithvale	Activists	23.83	5.08	12	20.08	7.71	13	22.57	6.88	7
	Nonactivists	15.67	7.10	3	22.06	6.66	17	17.92	8.68	13
Burgess	Activists	22.00	4.32	7	17.40	6.95	5	24.60	7.60	5
	Nonactivists	19.00	5.79	9	19.57	7.13	30	19.67	5.49	18
Camden	Activists	20.64	5.23	22	24.30	5.60	10	16.50	4.63	8
	Nonactivists	18.00	9.90	2	21.00	6.43	26	19.00	7.17	21
		GZTS-S[b]								
Smithvale	Activists	20.36	5.35	11	16.00	8.43	9	17.20	8.32	5
	Nonactivists	13.00	9.54	3	17.85	5.83	13	13.11	7.49	9
Burgess	Activists	20.60	3.85	5	16.00	8.76	4	21.25	4.86	4
	Nonactivists	17.83	5.38	6	17.62	6.73	26	18.19	5.12	16
Camden	Activists	18.60	5.44	15	21.20	5.92	10	11.83	6.59	6
	Nonactivists	25.00	0.00	1	19.50	7.06	22	17.63	8.57	19

					SIV-B[c]				
Smithvale	Activists	22.75	3.44	12	18.39	4.87	13	15.57	6.93	7
	Nonactivists	23.00	2.00	3	18.35	4.91	17	13.77	5.12	13
Burgess	Activists	20.29	3.04	7	21.60	3.51	5	14.40	6.23	5
	Nonactivists	21.00	4.42	9	19.00	4.87	30	14.78	5.61	18
Camden	Activists	21.00	3.44	22	16.50	6.01	10	13.50	10.18	8
	Nonactivists	18.50	0.71	2	17.48	5.27	27	15.67	5.94	21

[a] Normative data from 4,518 male and 1,329 female college students (Gordon, 1963a) indicate percentile ranks as follows: 6 (males), 8 (females) = 1st percentile; 23 (males), 24 (females) = 53rd and 51st percentile, respectively; 34 (males), 35 (females) = 99th percentile.

[b] Normative data from 912 college students (Guilford and Zimmerman, 1949) indicate a mean score of 18.8 and a standard deviation of 6.56.

[c] Normative data from 1,075 male and 746 female college students (Gordon, 1960) indicate percentile ranks as follows: 2 (males), 5 (females) = 1st percentile; 14 (males), 19 (females) = 50th and 48th percentile, respectively; 30 (males and females) = 99th percentile.

within an individual, it may be reasonable to expect it to be a factor leading him to espouse a political philosophy that is globally socially oriented, whereas a person who possesses little social concern might reasonably be expected to be led toward a political ideology that values individual gain even if, as occurs in a competitive system, it is at the expense of others.

Ascendancy and assertiveness

Both the Gordon Personal Profile Ascendancy Scale and Guilford-Zimmerman Temperament Survey Ascendancy-Submissiveness Scale purport to measure assertiveness and activity in groups. The data for both measures, reported in Table 16, indicate that the activists were significantly higher on this trait than the nonactivists. The Survey of Interpersonal Values Leadership Scale measures *valuing* leadership, as opposed to *practicing* it by being socially ascendant. The results of this scale, also included in Table 16, reveal, again, that activists were higher in this property than were nonactivists. There was also an ideology effect for the Leadership Scale which was due to the right-wing students valuing leadership more than either the middle-of-the-road students or the left-wing students.

A personality characteristic that it would seem logical for student political activists to possess is one of assertiveness and activity in groups, for it is through concerted group effort that specific social aims are sought by activist students. The findings from the measures of this attribute strongly imply that activist students do, indeed, possess this personality quality to a greater extent than do politically nonactive students.

It was also found that left and center students value

leadership less than do right students. An interesting behavioral demonstration of this among the left activists occurred on every campus. As was mentioned in Chapter 5, each left activist group on each campus denied (apparently independently) the existence and the relevance of leadership designations within their organizations. It would seem that the preference for participatory democracy so often expressed among student left activists runs deep and is a reflection of a more basic motivational tendency among leftist students in general to devalue leadership. Conversely, the predilection for strong authority frequently ascribed to rightists (Kerpelman, 1968) seems to be congruent with *their* motivational tendency to value leadership and power, as was found here.

Levelheadedness

In attempting to come up with a term to characterize the related personal properties of responsibility, restraint, perseverance, and objectivity, I could think of no term better than "levelheadedness." Several scales appeared to measure subsidiary properties of this characteristic. The Gordon Personal Profile Responsibility Scale measured responsibility and perseverance. The Guilford-Zimmerman Temperament Survey Restraint-Impulsiveness Scale measured seriousness of purpose and persistence. And the Guilford-Zimmerman Objectivity-Subjectivity Scale measured the qualities of being "thickskinned" and relatively insensitive versus being hypersensitive and suspicious. Descriptive data for these scales are presented in Table 17. Neither the Responsibility Scale nor the Restraint-Impulsiveness Scale yielded any significant differences among any of the groups.

The Objectivity-Subjectivity Scale yielded several signif-

TABLE 16. Descriptive data for ascendancy and assertiveness measures.

Institution	Activism	Left			Middle			Right		
		M	SD	N	M	SD	N	M	SD	N
					GPP-A[a]					
Smithvale	Activists	27.50	6.04	12	23.85	7.48	13	22.29	6.78	7
	Nonactivists	21.67	7.51	3	23.06	6.46	17	21.15	9.12	13
Burgess	Activists	27.14	6.23	7	22.00	7.65	5	25.00	9.33	5
	Nonactivists	18.78	5.97	9	22.23	6.65	30	21.33	4.34	18
Camden	Activists	25.86	5.53	22	27.40	3.75	10	19.75	5.09	8
	Nonactivists	20.00	11.31	2	20.15	6.00	26	20.62	6.24	21
					GZTS-A[b]					
Smithvale	Activists	19.00	6.02	11	16.20	6.36	10	14.00	5.72	4
	Nonactivists	13.33	5.13	3	14.87	5.15	15	13.00	5.92	9
Burgess	Activists	17.17	3.43	6	19.20	7.82	5	23.00	8.19	5
	Nonactivists	13.14	5.18	7	17.15	5.82	26	16.11	4.32	18
Camden	Activists	20.06	6.39	18	20.90	4.41	10	15.13	4.26	8
	Nonactivists	16.50	9.19	2	15.75	5.96	20	13.68	6.35	19

Ideology

SIV-L[c]

Smithvale	Activists	12.67	3.99	12	14.23	5.78	13	15.71	5.82	7
	Nonactivists	16.00	3.46	3	11.88	3.43	17	14.39	8.33	13
Burgess	Activists	12.14	3.93	7	14.00	4.00	5	20.20	6.87	5
	Nonactivists	10.89	2.76	9	13.53	5.98	30	15.78	6.06	18
Camden	Activists	12.09	4.24	22	18.30	5.76	10	19.63	4.21	8
	Nonactivists	12.00	0.00	2	10.70	6.79	27	12.52	6.96	21

[a] Normative data from 4,518 male and 1,329 female college students (Gordon, 1963a) indicate percentile ranks as follows: 7 (males), 6 (females) = 1st percentile; 22 (males and females) = 50th and 52nd percentile, respectively; 33 (males and females) = 99th percentile.

[b] Normative data from 912 college students (Guilford and Zimmerman, 1949) indicate a mean score of 15.0 and a standard deviation of 5.82.

[c] Normative data from 1,075 male and 746 female college students (Gordon, 1960) indicate percentile ranks as follows: 2 (males), 1 (females) = 1st percentile; 18 (males), 11 (females) = 50th and 48th percentile, respectively; 32 (males), 29 (females) = 99th percentile.

TABLE 17. Descriptive data for levelheadedness measures.

Institution	Activism	Ideology								
		Left			Middle			Right		
		M	SD	N	M	SD	N	M	SD	N
					GPP-R[a]					
Smithvale	Activists	20.50	3.80	12	21.92	6.61	13	24.43	5.50	7
	Nonactivists	25.67	2.08	3	18.35	6.54	17	20.00	6.34	13
Burgess	Activists	21.29	5.77	7	24.60	2.07	5	25.80	6.57	5
	Nonactivists	18.89	5.65	9	21.87	6.83	30	22.56	8.56	18
Camden	Activists	18.41	3.67	22	22.50	3.95	10	20.75	10.90	8
	Nonactivists	20.50	0.71	2	22.46	5.78	26	23.62	5.64	21
					GZTS-R[b]					
Smithvale	Activists	19.55	2.21	11	19.90	5.34	10	17.67	4.93	6
	Nonactivists	22.00	2.65	3	15.73	5.09	15	17.86	5.24	7
Burgess	Activists	22.17	3.19	6	21.00	2.00	5	17.00	4.06	5
	Nonactivists	15.86	6.23	7	17.54	3.60	24	19.06	3.44	16
Camden	Activists	15.50	3.90	16	17.20	4.96	10	16.00	5.43	8
	Nonactivists	18.00	0.00	1	16.76	3.65	21	16.33	5.61	21

GZTS-O[c]

Smithvale	Activists	17.50	6.10	10	17.09	5.52	11	18.00	6.00	7
	Nonactivists	18.00	1.73	3	19.27	4.45	15	16.44	5.77	9
Burgess	Activists	19.33	3.50	6	20.50	3.11	4	12.60	1.82	5
	Nonactivists	15.17	1.72	6	16.88	4.41	24	17.31	4.63	16
Camden	Activists	16.69	4.39	13	14.33	6.61	9	18.63	6.32	8
	Nonactivists	0.00	0.00	1	15.55	4.99	22	17.45	5.39	20

[a]Normative data from 4,518 male and 1,329 female college students (Gordon, 1963a) indicate percentile ranks as follows: 9 (males and females) = 1st percentile; 24 (males and females) = 53rd and 55th percentile, respectively; 34 (males and females) = 99th percentile.
[b]Normative data from 912 college students (Guilford and Zimmerman, 1949) indicate a mean score of 16.4 and a standard deviation of 4.89.
[c]Normative data from 912 college students (Guilford and Zimmerman, 1949) indicate a mean score of 17.4 and a standard deviation of 5.18.

icant differences. Middle- and right-oriented students were, on the whole, more objective and "thickskinned" than left-oriented students.[5] The Institution X Activism X Ideology interaction of the Guilford-Zimmerman Objectivity-Subjectivity Scale is plotted in Figure 4.

Radical left students have been characterized sometimes in the mass media as irresponsible and impulsive, and, indeed, some empirical evidence supports this. For example, Whittaker and Watts (1971) found that Berkeley left activists, as contrasted with randomly selected students, were significantly less self-controlled and less ordered, and significantly more labile, more aggressive, and more exhibitionistic. There are, no doubt, irresponsible and impulsive persons in any group, and these may be the ones who attract mass media

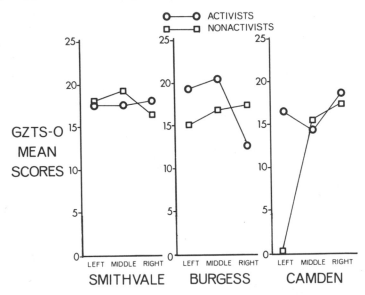

FIGURE 4. Guilford-Zimmerman Temperament Survey Objectivity-Subjectivity Scale, Institution X Activism X Ideology interaction.

attention. The measures of these characteristics as personality tendencies in the present research, on a broad sample of left activists, did not lend support to this view, however. Just as left activists or right activists cannot be characterized, on the basis of the present research findings, as being more or less intelligent or more or less emotionally stable than each other or than other student groups, neither can their personality functioning be characterized as being more or less irresponsible or impulsive.

The leftists (activists and nonactivists alike) *can* be viewed, in general, as being more subjective, hypersensitive, and "thinskinned" than either the moderates or the rightists. Other investigators have reported similar findings for left activists. Winborn and Jansen (1967), for example, found that student leaders of liberal sociopolitical organizations tend to be more emotionally sensitive, and Cowdry, Keniston, and Cabin (1970) reported that anti-Vietnam War students at Yale viewed themselves as significantly more passionate and significantly less realistic than did pro-War students. Perhaps this hypersensitivity and greater openness to the feeling-tone of surrounding events may be one of the factors contributing to the adherence to a leftist ideology by some students. That is, students who come to adopt a leftist world view may do so because they are more sensitive (or hypersensitive) to injustices and may therefore choose to embrace a political philosophy that espouses rapid social amelioration. Moderates and rightists, on the other hand, because they are more "thickskinned" and less sensitive, may not see the need for such broad social change and may thus come to embrace a philosophy that seeks to change the status quo more slowly or to maintain it. Schiff (1964) characterized right activists as being concerned with control over impulse expression. Placing this in a comparative context, the present results suggest that his finding can be extended to right students in general.

Supplementary Findings

Commitment

In Chapter 1 it was suggested that one variable to examine in the activism phenomenon is the variable of commitment, and it was indicated that other investigators (Keniston, 1968; Sampson, 1967) have pointed to its possible relevance in the study of student activism. I had planned in this study to evaluate commitment by observing differences in responses between leaders of the various activist organizations and members of the organizations. As it turned out, the plans to examine the data in this way had to be abandoned, for, as was indicated above, the left activists did not make leader-follower distinctions. Circumstances presented themselves, however, such that a more direct behavioral measure of commitment could be obtained among the members of at least one group, the left activists at the University of Camden. As was mentioned in Chapter 3, a considerable amount of turmoil gripped the Camden campus during the period that this study was being conducted there. During the demonstrations, in which many of the left activists who were studied in this investigation participated, the students were allowed to demonstrate outside of a police-cordoned university building. If the students chose to cross the police lines, though, they faced arrest. The students were thus given a clear choice: to participate actively in a protest activity, or to express a further commitment as well by voluntarily subjecting themselves to arrest.

The act of submitting voluntarily to arrest served as a good behavioral criterion of commitment, I felt. Consequently, when the research questionnaires were administered to the left activist students at Camden, they were asked to indicate on their Code Number Instructions, by placing a special code digit in the "Membership" space, whether or not they had been arrested during the recent demonstrations.[6] While the arrest designations are self-report data and are possibly subject to the "impression-giving" pitfall concerning these kinds of data that I discussed previously, I felt that a comparative analysis of the characteristics of the voluntary arrestees versus the other members might still shed some light on the commitment variable.

The descriptive and questionnaire data for the voluntary arrestees, compared with those of the Camden left activists who were not arrested, are presented in Tables 18 and 19. Of all these measures, only one yielded a statistically significant difference between the voluntary arrestees and the other members. As measured by the Activity-Actual Scale, the arrestees were more politically active than the non-arrestees. Hence, although there was a distinct behavioral definition of

TABLE 18. Descriptive data for major and sex of Camden left activists.

Variable	Voluntary arrestees	Other members
Major		
No. biological, natural, physical sciences	0	1
No. business, engineering	0	0
No. arts, humanities, social sciences	7	12
No. education	0	1
No. other	1	0
Sex		
No. males	4	7
No. females	4	7

commitment (submitting to arrest) present in at least one of the left activist groups, almost no differences were found

TABLE 19. Descriptive data for demographic information and questionnaire data of Camden left activists.

Variable	Voluntary arrestees		Other members		t
	M	SD	M	SD	(two-tailed)
Demographic					
Age	21.75	2.96	20.43	1.65	1.28
Year in school	3.25	1.28	3.29	1.20	0.07
Year at institution	4.00	2.39	2.86	1.29	1.39
Number of activities	1.62	1.32	2.14	1.06	0.96
Criterion					
PEC	1.69	0.64	1.84	0.38	0.68
ACT-A	49.38	7.85	41.29	7.51	2.28*
ACT-D	53.38	7.39	50.43	6.85	0.90
Personality, intellectual					
QWT	61.75	12.93	58.57	15.91	0.47
CTAA	21.38	3.02	21.14	2.66	0.19
GPP-E	21.50	5.13	23.29	6.50	0.64
GZTS-E	16.67	6.65	15.82	4.92	0.28
SIV-R	7.50	2.45	7.64	2.34	0.13
SIV-S	16.75	3.15	17.29	2.20	0.45
SIV-C	6.25	3.28	5.14	1.99	0.94
SIV-I	26.75	3.62	26.29	3.32	0.29
GPP-S	22.00	5.61	19.86	5.05	0.88
GZTS-S	21.40	3.85	17.20	5.73	1.38
SIV-B	19.75	2.82	21.71	3.65	1.25
GPP-A	28.25	4.50	24.50	5.75	1.52
GZTS-A	22.86	5.24	18.27	6.63	1.46
SIV-L	12.63	5.95	11.79	3.12	0.41
GPP-R	18.75	3.88	18.21	3.68	0.31
GZTS-R	16.29	3.55	14.89	4.26	0.66
GZTS-O	19.00	3.56	15.67	4.50	1.20

Note.—N = 8 and 14 for the voluntary arrestees and the other members, respectively, except for the GZTS E, A, S, R, and O Scales, where N = 6, 11; 7, 11; 5, 10; 7, 9; and 4, 9, respectively.
*$p < .05$.

between highly committed left activists and their less committed fellow left activists. The only differentiating variable was one that might be expected most, namely, activism. In this group of left activists, the students who were most active in radical activities were willing to demonstrate their commitment by their actions. The failure to find any other differences between highly committed and less committed left activists thus fails to support the speculations about correlates of commitment that Keniston (1968) and Sampson (1967) have suggested might exist.

"Factors" differentiating groups

We have examined separately each measure administered to the students and seen in what way, if any, the various groups differed from each other. In a research effort such as this one, in which many measures are administered to many groups, an additional way to examine the same data is to determine the extent to which, and the manner in which, the groups of subjects may be differentiated by the same set of variables operating together. More simply put, the question is: What *combinations* of variables differentiate among the groups? This question can be answered by way of a multiple discriminant analysis, an operation which orders the research groups on a set of derived "factors." Such an analysis was performed on the 17 questionnaire scales unrelated to the criteria of activism and ideology. The student groups were combined across institutions for the purpose of this analysis, that is, the analysis was designed to yield descriptions of the six activism-ideology groups.

The multiple discriminant analysis resulted in five roots, or "factors," but the first two "factors" were the ones with the most statistical validity.[7] Correlations of the 17 variables with each discriminant function, or "factor," are presented in Table 20. Group centroids for these factors are presented in Table 21.

"Factor 1" has been entitled an "Authoritarianism" factor. As seen from Table 20, the Survey of Interpersonal Values Benevolence Scale correlates most highly but in a *negative* direction, with this function. The Survey of Interpersonal Values Conformity Scale loads in a *positive* direction next most highly on this factor. The remaining variables correlate negligibly with this function. In general, the rightist students are highest on this "Authoritarianism" factor (see Figure 5). Both the right activists and the right nonactivists differed significantly from each other and from the other four groups, as can be seen in Figure 5. Next in order were the center-ideology groups, and then came the left groups. The left activists were significantly lower on this factor than all

TABLE 20. Correlations of measures with the discriminant functions.

| Measure | Discriminant function | | | | |
	1	2	3	4	5
QWT	-.08	-.07	.10	.20	-.11
CTAA	.20	.02	.01	.42	-.40
GPP-E	-.02	.06	.29	-.17	-.23
GZTS-E	.22	.09	.34	-.18	.21
SIV-R	.31	-.57	.42	.32	.20
SIV-S	-.18	-.61	-.07	-.24	.15
SIV-C	.39	.20	.13	-.35	.19
SIV-I	-.14	.28	-.35	-.39	-.53
GPP-S	-.13	.20	.22	.08	.39
GZTS-S	-.06	-.13	.24	-.03	.12
SIV-B	-.61	.04	-.20	.27	.16
GPP-A	-.32	.45	.54	.16	.08
GZTS-A	-.13	.30	.38	.23	.07
SIV-L	.34	.46	.19	.36	-.11
GPP-R	.26	.03	.14	.19	-.11
GZTS-R	.05	.17	.22	.31	-.06
GZTS-O	.25	.09	.20	-.08	.20

TABLE 21. Group centroids of the discriminant functions.

Group	Discriminant function				
	1	2	3	4	5
Left activists	22.69	-32.17	36.33	-25.81	-38.21
Middle activists	26.37	-32.94	37.13	-23.93	-38.22
Right activists	30.27	-31.23	35.66	-25.38	-38.07
Left nonactivists	24.71	-33.49	34.58	-24.73	-38.42
Middle nonactivists	26.17	-33.76	36.09	-25.50	-38.05
Right nonactivists	28.20	-33.36	36.44	-25.91	-38.34

the other groups, whereas the left nonactivists did not differ significantly from the middle nonactivists. There were, in other words, three extreme groups on this factor: the right activists and right nonactivists were highest, and the left activists, lowest.

I have called "Factor 2" an "Autonomy" factor. The Survey of Interpersonal Values Recognition and Support Scales correlate highest and in a negative direction with this function, the Survey of Interpersonal Values Leadership and Gordon Personal Profile Ascendancy Scales correlate next highest and in a positive direction, and the Guilford-Zimmerman Temperament Survey Ascendance-Submissiveness Scale correlates next highest and also positively with this function, as is indicated in Table 20. The group centroids of "Factor 2" are presented in Table 21, and in Figure 5 is presented the results of the analysis of the group differences. The activists in general were higher on this function. Of the activists, the right and left activists were higher than the other subgroups, while not differing significantly from each other, on this factor.

These multiple discriminant analysis group "profiles" tend to reinforce some of the findings examined in the scale-by-scale discussion above. They support the thesis that rightists must be able to tolerate contradictions—or at least to so

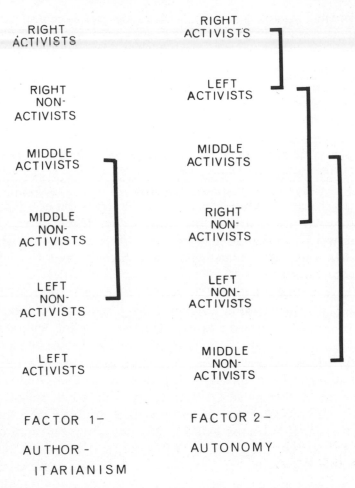

FACTOR 1 −

AUTHOR -

ITARIANISM

FACTOR 2 −

AUTONOMY

FIGURE 5. Differences on each discriminant analysis factor among activism-ideology groups. (No significant differences among groups connected by brackets.)

compartmentalize them that they do not appear as contradictions. On both of the seemingly opposite significant factors resulting from the discriminant analysis, the "Authoritarianism" factor and the "Autonomy" factor, the right activists were the highest group. The term "obedient rebels," coined by Schiff (1964) to characterize these apparently contradictory tendencies in right activists, appears to have some empirical substance, then.

The multiple discriminant analysis also supports the thesis that leftists do not value conformity or recognition but do value independence or autonomy highly. That they do is consistent with the findings of others who have investigated left activists (Haan, Smith, and Block, 1968; Whittaker and Watts, 1971). The overall consistency of these findings suggests that this constellation of nonauthoritarian and autonomous orientations is perhaps more uniquely characteristic of leftist students than is any other set of personal qualities. The independent thinking and nonconformity characteristics postulated as properties of the student left (Sampson, 1967) are thus probably valid ones which likely have personality and attitudinal bases.

Replication

Subsequent to the completion of this research, and completely independent of it, a replication and extension of it was undertaken (Abramowitz, 1972). Abramowitz's study was conducted at a large university in the Rocky Mountain area. It extended the present study by including a third group along the activism dimension—nonjoining students who did not belong to any campus organizations, political or nonpolitical—and by including some different measures of competence and adjustment. Neither of these extensions need concern us here: the discussion below focuses on those aspects of the Abramowitz study that are comparable to those reported in this book.

Using the Activity Scale, Abramowitz (1972) found essentially the same results, for both the Activism-Actual and the Activism-Desired subscales, as those obtained in this investigation. This provides additional support for the validity of the Activity Scale, as well as support for the generalizations about activism among student groups made above. Abramowitz's data on intelligence also supported the findings of this study. He found no differences among ideology groups, no differences among comparable activism groups, and no activism-ideology subgroup differences that would indicate that any particular subgroup possessed greater intelligence. That differences in intelligence were found between the nonjoiners (not comparable to any activism level in the present study) and the other main activism levels suggests that the intelligence measuring instruments (the same ones used in this study) were sensitive to differences in intelligence if they were there. Similarly, with the two measures of personality that were the same as those used in this study—the Gordon Personal Profile Emotional Stability Scale and Responsibility Scale—Abramowitz found, as was also found here, no differences among groups that were comparable to those in the present study. Again, he did find differences between nonjoiners and the other activism groups that would suggest that these scales could detect differences when they existed.

Essentially, then, many of the findings of this study were obtained on an entirely different sample by an independent investigator. The results of this study thus take on added significance in light of Abramowitz's (1972) replication.

From the outset, this research was concerned, in part, with attempting to overcome some of the problems of previous investigations in the area of student activism. Like most investigations, though, this one was also an imperfect instrument. A deliberate attempt was made to minimize every potential problem; still, some problems remain with this research. Before considering what some of the implications of the research findings are, we should first discuss some important considerations to bear in mind in dealing with those implications.

Considerations

Asserting "no differences"

The first consideration is a statistical-experimental design one. Statistically significant results tell us that the probability is small (in this research, the odds were less than five in a hundred) that a difference among groups could have occurred by chance. We can "say something," with only a small chance of being incorrect, about statistically significant differences among groups, but we cannot with equal assuredness "say something" about results that are not statistically significant. Failure to find significant differences among groups on certain of the measures in this research does not mean that the differences are not there, for it may be that our instruments may not have been fine enough to find them or that our sampling was imprecise enough to obscure them. Hence the failure to find significant differences among any of the activism-ideology subgroups on some of the measures used in this research (on such variables as intelligence, emotional stability, or responsibility) does not necessarily mean that a "true" difference among the groups does not exist.

It was because some of the research questions may have implicitly posited the "null hypothesis" (the hypothesis that no "true" differences exist between two groups on some measure) that care was taken to choose the measuring instruments and to sample groups as carefully as possible. In almost all cases, the questionnaires selected for inclusion in the research were those which have undergone extensive testing of their validity and reliability. In addition, for many personality and intellectual properties, two questionnaire scales, rather than one, were given to the students to measure the trait in question. One can be somewhat more confident in accepting a result of no sigificant differences if two independent scales measuring the same personal property are included, as was the case with intelligence, emotional stability, and responsibility, than if only one instrument was the sole basis for the findings. Furthermore, if no significant differences were found for one scale of a multiscale questionnaire, the fact that other scales of that same instrument did yield group differences would suggest that the overall instrument is a viable one and that some confidence can be placed in the failure to find group differences. Finally, independent replication of findings of no difference, as discussed in the previous chapter, add some confidence to the validity of those findings.

In regard to sampling procedures, care was taken to sample the participating students as rigorously as possible. Institutions which did not have viable left, middle, and right activist organizations on campus were not selected for study. On the campuses that were selected, activist students were assigned to an ideology subcategory not only on the basis of their organization membership, but also on the basis of their scoring in a congruent fashion on an instrument measuring their liberalness-conservativeness. The data of any students who were inconsistent were eliminated from further consideration. A quantitative check of the activism dimension was made as well, by use of an instrument to measure activism. Withal, we cannot *assert* the null hypothesis—wherever negative findings occur, the evidence can only *suggest* that the various subgroups may not truly differ in the variable under consideration.

Measurement

The main results of this study are embodied in the questionnaire findings. While all of the questionnaires were self-report instruments, and may thus appear to be subject to the problems inherent in self-reports, several of them (such as the Survey of Interpersonal Values and the Gordon Personal Profile) did have anti-faking devices built into them. These two instruments also used a forced-choice format, which was designed to make the traits being measured less obvious to the respondent, and therefore to circumvent possible attempts to appear consistent with some public image. Other instruments (the Quick Word Test and the Control Test AA) assessed factual information. Consequently, most of the properties measured in this investigation were probably not, to any great extent, influenced by conscious effort on the part of the respondents to appear in a desired light. It is important to note this because, while the methodology of this investigation did not allow selection of all students without their being aware of the reason for their selection (as was suggested as being desirable by Geller and Howard, 1969), it is unlikely that much faking of personality and other traits could have occurred anyway. The anonymity stressed throughout the research procedures probably also helped to minimize students' attempts to influence the direction of their responses.

Sampling

It is hoped that the stringent criteria used for assignment of students to each of the research cells resulted in relatively "pure" activism-ideology subgroups. The Politico-Economic Conservatism Scale and the Activity Scale used to assess these dimensions assured that the subgroups would cover the range of political ideologies and of political activity levels. On the other hand, this procedure entailed the exclusion of those activist students whose ideology was inconsistent with that of the activist organization to which they belonged. For example, students who joined a left activist organization for other than leftist ideological motivations were not included in this study. The results that were obtained, therefore, reflect the motivational, personality, intelligence, and demographic characteristics of ideologically consistent activist students, not all activist students. Cowdry, Keniston, and Cabin (1970) have compared ideologically consistent students with ideologically inconsistent students, and the reader is referred to their paper for an interesting discussion of this issue.

For this research, I have sampled students, organizations, and institutions. Of students, there were originally 291, of organizations (activism-ideology subgroups) there were 18, but of instutitions, there were only 3. Obviously, the findings in regard to the institutional differences can be generalized much less accurately than can the findings related to activism and to ideology, and for this reason, discussion of the inter-institutional differences that were found have been under-played. The three institutions, while perhaps exemplary, only loosely can be considered representative of all institutions of their kind. Insofar as institution type may influence the development of students' personality and political attitudes, the three institutions may be considered as tentative "natural" experiments. It remains, however, for a much larger national survey, ranging across a much larger number of institutions of higher education, such as Astin (1968) has undertaken, to produce firmer generalizations about the interactive effect of institutions on students' activism, on their ideology, and on the numerous psychological character-istics examined in the present study.

No conclusions concerning the interactions of ethnic, religious, socioeconomic, and family background character-istics of the groups studied in this research with the psychological variables studied can be reached from this research endeavor. Again, Astin (1968) has been able to do this within the purview of his large national study of college students, as has Braungart (1966) on a more limited scale. This was not the focus of the present research, however. To have attempted in this research to have included enough students to be able to examine the interactive effects of the sociological variables mentioned with the psychological variables actually examined would have extended its scope beyond reasonable limits.

I think it is important for the reader to keep the above

considerations in mind as we next discuss the broader implications of this study. No research program is without faults, and undoubtedly there are other flaws I have failed to mention. Consideration of the implications of this study should be tempered by its shortcomings.

Implications

Although this investigation was not guided by specific hypotheses, rigorously stated and precisely testable, it was motivated by certain questions about the student activism movement and about college students generally. Let us now return to the questions posed in Chapter 2 and see what answers have been revealed by this investigation. With the caveats expressed in the section immediately above, it would be more circumspect to call them "suggestions to answers," but in any case, let us turn to the implications of the findings for the questions that were raised.

Activists and ideologists

The first question posed was:

What are the comparative demographic, ability, personality, and value characteristics of American college students who engage in different levels of political activism? Specifically, is the politically active student a different sort of person from the politically nonactive student?

A good way to summarize both of these questions is to ask: Given that social conditions are such as to arouse some students to protest or to engage in activity focused upon the sociopolitical situation, why is it that only some students do so? The personality characteristics that predispose some students to engage in sociopolitical activity seem to be, from the results of this study, the same no matter what the students' political ideology. Left activists, who aim at *radically changing* the social and political structure mainly by working upon it, center activists, who predominantly aim toward *gradually improving* that structure by working within it, and right activists, who aim predominantly toward *strictly keeping* societal structures from changing rapidly by working within the structure, are more similar in their personality characteristics than they are different. Likewise, the personal and social qualities of college students who are not aroused to extraordinary political action also seem to be more similar than different, no matter what their political ideology. Activists are, obviously, more politically active than non-activists, and they also desire to be even more politically active than nonactivists. Political activists tend to engage in more campus activities of all kinds than do nonpolitical, nonactivist students, and they tend to be younger. Activists value leadership more, tend to be more sociable, are definitely more ascendant and assertive, and are less needful of support and encouragement than are nonactivists. They tend to be high in a factor I have labeled "Autonomy." Activists and nonactivists do not appear to differ from each other on emotional stability, intellectual ability, or restraint and responsibility, but for the most part, activists and nonactivists (ideology aside) are different sorts of people from each other.

The next set of questions posed concerned the same factors, but in regard to ideology, rather than activism.

What are the comparative demographic, ability, personality, and value characteristics of American college students who espouse different political ideologies? Specifically, how do the little-studied students on the right of the political spectrum compare with their more intensively studied counterparts on the left? And what is the middle-of-the-road student population like?

In answer to these questions, the findings show that leftists (activists and nonactivists alike) tend to be high in political activity as well as in the desire to engage in political activity. They value independence highly, as well as benevolence. On the other hand, student leftists value recognition, conformity, and leadership little. They tend to be subjective rather than objective. On a factor labeled "Authoritarianism," they are quite low. Student leftists tend to be older also. Student rightists, not too surprisingly, are almost opposite the leftists on most of the personality traits on which ideology groups differed. They tend to be less politically active and to express little desire to be more active, and they value benevolence relatively little. Student rightists value conformity and leadership highly, value recognition, and are more objective in their thinking. Only in terms of independence are student rightists similar to student leftists, for both value this quality. Student rightists are more likely to be male than female. Middle-of-the-road students, true to the label, more often than not tend to fall between the extremes on the measured characteristics, and when they tend toward an extreme on a personal attribute, they are likely to share that characteristic as often with leftists as with rightists. Moderates are moderately politically active, and they express only a moderate desire to engage in political activity. They are moderately benevolent. They value conformity and leadership little, but they also value independence little. They value recognition highly, and they are objective in their thinking. The different ideologists do not differ in intelligence, adjustment, or restraint.

Thus, the answer to the questions about ideologists is that, in several respects, students holding different political ideologies differ in their personality makeup. This research endeavor has pointed to several personality and attitudinal variables that are differentially associated with left, middle, and right ideologies among American students in institutions of higher education: social acceptance concern, valuing leadership, benevolence, and objectivity. The ideologically left students, activists and nonactivists alike, perhaps most cogently (albeit simplistically) may be characterized as "soft-headed and soft-hearted," while ideologically right students, just as exaggeratedly, may be characterized as "hard-headed and hard-hearted." This global picture supports Keniston's (1969) notion that "Moral issues are central to student radicalism [p. 32]," for "soft-headed and soft-hearted" implies a kind of humanistic moral concern, while the opposite implies a relative lack of moral concern. Haan, Smith, and Block (1968) have in fact demonstrated that, in part, principled moral concerns are associated with a tendency to engage in left-oriented protest.

Given these communalities within ideological groups, the related issues still arise as to why some leftist students engage in radical left political activity and others do not, why some middle-of-the-road students seek campus office while others do not, and why some rightist students identify themselves with conservative organizations whereas others do not. Keniston (1969) has echoed this concern by pointing out that ". . . for every activist, there are many others who share his belief but do not act. . . . As yet, little is known about the psychological and social processes by which individuals are activated . . . [p. 32]."

It is evident that there are many determinants of political behavior other than purely psychological ones—socialization practices, political philosophy, and economic concerns, to name a few. Even though the present study examined an extensive set of personality variables, it generally did not find any personal characteristics that distinguished between activists and nonactivists within left, within center, or within right ideology groups. Keniston (1969) has suggested that psychological explanations by themselves are inadequate, and that moral issues ought to be investigated as well, as Haan, Smith, and Block (1968), for example, have done fruitfully. Certainly it makes sense to look at these and other (political, environmental, etc.) factors, for the clearer explanation of any social phenomenon will come from a multitude of approaches, not from an exclusive one.

Uniqueness of left activists

We have been able to point to numerous psychological correlates on which student activists and nonactivists differ, and on which left ideologists, center ideologists, and right ideologists vary. Yet, none of the individual personality measures (save for "desired activism," which only very broadly can be considered a personality measure) yielded differences among the six activism-ideology subgroups. The answer, then, to the question:

Are left activists, in particular, unique in any way, or do the personal qualities ascribed to them characterize the involved generally or leftists generally?

must be that student left activists are not unique or special psychologically. This is perhaps the most important general result emerging from this research. Although we cannot assert the conclusion of no "true" differences with complete assurance, the thrust of the findings of this study suggests, as has been suggested elsewhere (Abramowitz, 1972; Block, Haan, and Smith, 1969; Kerpelman, 1969b; Lipset, 1968), that personal qualities usually imputed to student left activists characterize the involved generally (no matter what their ideology) or leftists generally (no matter what their level of political involvement). The present findings further suggest that previous speculative and investigative endeavors that have attributed certain characteristics to left activist students probably have done so incorrectly, as a result of the failure to separate activism from ideology. In the present research, only on lack of "Authoritarianism," a combination of personality characteristics, did the left activists stand out psychologically from the other groups. On the "Autonomy" factor, interestingly, the left activists and the right activists stood together. In not one of the many separate demographic, intelligence, or personality measures, however, were student left activists appreciably different from any other subgroup, nor were right activists, nor were any activism-ideology subgroups.[1]

Even within the attribute of commitment among left activists, for which there was in this research a strong behavioral index, there were no major differences between highly committed left activists and their less committed confreres. Prior conjecture which has suggested that among left activists there is a special subgroup whose high commitment is correlated with unusual, and unusually positive, personality characteristics (Keniston, 1968; Sampson, 1967) was not borne out.

As a result of recent events, much attention has been focused upon radical left student activists in institutions of higher education in the United States. They have been romanticized as psychological noblemen in some quarters and deprecated as psychological misfits in others. Yet the results of this investigation do not indicate that student left activists are unique in any of the psychological attributes studied. Left activists are not psychological supermen, the present results suggest. Recognition of this seems to be increasing gradually in academic circles. The candid remarks of the President of Harvard, Nathn Pusey, at that institution's 1970 commencement, to the effect that campus activists are neither better nor worse than their campus contemporaries, is one illustration of this. An asute journalistic account of the people and events leading to the 1969 Harvard student strike, written by a participant observer of the Harvard student scene (Kelman, 1970), also points to the many negative personality and moral qualities embodied in some of the radical left activists, as well as to the positive features of these same people and of other student strikers. Knott's (1971) review of the research literature on student activists also takes note of the negative as well as the positive qualities among student left activists and points to their relative nonuniqueness. In an empirical study of the moral reasoning of student left activists, Haan, Smith, and Block (1968) pointed out that this group contained not only students at one of the highest levels of moral development, but that left activists also included among their number a substantial portion of people who were at one of the lowest levels of moral development. All of this simply illustrates a point made many years ago by one of the most radical left thinkers of all that revolutionary movements contain the best of people but also the worst of people (Lenin, 1964).

The myth of the psychological uniqueness of student left activists should be laid to rest, for it no longer holds, if it ever did. The activist student left in American higher education should be understood for what it really is, not what overzealous (both positive and negative) commentators would have us believe. These students are people, like the rest of their fellows in most respects, with the foibles and strengths shared by the rest of the college population. They do not differ from the rest of the college population on such important psychological variables as intelligence, emotional stability, and responsibility, and they are likely to possess their share of saints and sinners in equal proportion to the rest of the college population.

But "established fact" dies hard, and the overdrawn, romanticized earlier view of the activist student left probably still holds sway among many social scientists and among some segments of the broader public. This underlines the necessity of using caution in ascribing attributes to particular student groups when only the dimension of activism or only the dimension of ideology is taken into account. As we have seen, this is not merely an academic distinction, for the research which has been done, which has been disseminated subsequently via scholarly reviews (cf. Katz, 1967) and thence via the popular news media (cf. Leo, 1967), has frequently not made this distinction, and a probably inaccurate picture of today's college students has been the result.

The state of the campus

Finally, what do the demographic, ability, personality, and value characteristics of American college students suggest about institutions of higher education today, and what do these characteristics augur for the state of the student movement in the future?

If the samples in this research are at all representative, they indicate that students today tend to be more left-leaning than right-leaning in their thinking. Even student government bodies tend to fall to the left of center. Those students whose political ideology is at the left end of the spectrum tend to engage more in sociopolitical activism, whereas most students whose political orientation is to the right avoid organized public political activity, at least at the institutions studied here. Perhaps it is because left radicalism is in the public eye, reaches for and attains attention, that the campuses have stronger left than right activist movements. A student who is in the least inclined toward the philosophy and goals of the left can, at least on many college campuses, find publicly known organizations that espouse those ends. He can participate more easily in these organizations, and even more easily be a hanger-on in some of their activities. On the other hand, a student with a conservative philosophy may feel himself, on many campuses now, to be a stranger in a strange land. Few of his fellows espouse rightist beliefs, and fewer publicly organize around these beliefs. Consequently, a student rightist must have a fervently held ideology to face the opprobrium and scorn that accompanies going against the tide and becoming a right activist on most campuses.

Indeed, the increasingly broader base of the student left on American college campuses may possibly account for the failure to find psychological uniqueness in the student left today. It *is* possible that the students involved in the "new left" movement of the mid-1960's *did* possess exclusively the positive personal characteristics that were ascribed to them, but that now the movement's base has broadened so that less able and less psychologically rich students are included within student left activist groups. The unfortunate tendency in earlier research not to make appropriate comparisons nor to use appropriate measures prevents a definitive answer on this issue, and the tendency of earlier writers to make speculations based upon little or no solid information adds little light now. One thing that is clear, though, is that at this point in time, when appropriate comparisons are made and appropriate measures are used, student left activists do not appear to have an exclusive claim to the high levels of intelligence, the psychological richness, and the many other positive properties ascribed to them in earlier research.

From this, we can perhaps speculate about what this all means for the campuses for the immediate future. There are several factors that should enter into these speculations: a more broadly based student left now than before, possibly due to the greater ease of publicly identifying as a leftist; the concomitant dilution of the left, containing now not only highly committed members, but also many more students who are less committed and who are more ideologically inconsistent than those on the right; the personality qualities of independence shared by both left- and right-oriented students; the apparent lack of difference in the important variables of intelligence, emotional stability, and responsibility among the several activism-ideology groups on American campuses—indeed, the lack of psychological uniqueness among any of these groups. All of these factors seems to point to a resynthesis, an increased coming together, of the student bodies in American institutions of higher education after the polarization that occurred in the 1960's. On the left, one of the factors causing the dilution of extremism will probably continue to be the popularity of the left, with a consequent infusion into the New Left movement of students with more moderate viewpoints. As that occurs, perhaps the student right can begin to surface and, through their increased exposure, also begin to attract more moderate students.

To be sure, efforts at polarization, deliberate or tacit, are likely to continue to be made. But in the movement toward polarization, the follies of each pole are exposed more clearly, and having witnessed in the 1960's some of the disastrous results of extreme viewpoints, students in the 1970's will likely resist efforts toward extremism. This seemed to have occurred within the student left movement itself, where extreme actions led to disruption of classes, closing of buildings, and interference with what the bulk of the students wanted most, their education. A subsequent disenchantment with the extreme left resulted. On the right, resistance to extremism seemed to have been exemplified by the apparent rejection in the early 1970's, on the part of most students on campuses across the country, of one of the most widespread efforts in recent years by national political figures to polarize the populace. Young people were exhorted to actively reject the left, and were given implicit sanction by conservative political figures to isolate and crush the left on campuses and in society as a whole.

At the beginning of the 1970's, in other words, the sense and stability of most American college students seems to be prevailing. If I am allowed a prediction, it would be that the 1970's will see more tranquil campuses.

Concluding Comments

I wish to conclude this discussion of the implications of this research, and this book itself, with a plea, a plea for objectivity. Ever since the student activism phenomenon emerged (or more accurately, re-emerged) in recent years in the United States, article upon article, book upon book, and speech upon speech have been written about it. In a broad sense, one can fairly state that while the mass media and political figures in general have reacted negatively, or at least skeptically, to the left activist movement, social scientists in general have embraced it, or at least been sympathetic to it.[2] An unfortunate result of this has been that the mass media and political figures frequently expound anti-student sentiments, while the social science literature is full of apologia for the student movement. In their rush to print or to the spoken word, both camps have been long on conjecture and short on solid evidence. All of this has only added fuel to the fires of polarization.

Insofar as the mass media and politicians are concerned, this may be understandable (if not excusable), in that part of the task of these societal agencies is to express quickly their opinions on the meaning of current events. It is more serious and inexcusable, however, when premature speculation and overgeneralization occur in the social sciences, for as sciences, these disciplines are supposed to obtain and to weigh the evidence carefully, and to limit their generalizations to the evidence at hand. Yet time and again, social scientists have erred in this regard, as I attempted to show in Chapter 1, ignoring contradictory evidence and methodological inadequacies in investigations of left-wing activists. It is true that student left activists have sought positive changes in American society: the end to the seemingly futile Vietnam War, the end to secret research on campuses, and the establishment of a counterforce to the military-industrial complex, to name a few examples. But in generalizing from the students' positive goals to their psychological motivations, some social scientists have been influenced by a strong positive "halo" effect.

A slightly different discussion of the background for this "halo" effect has been offered by Blum (1969), who himself has been sympathetic toward the student left:

The importance of adjustment, of curiosity, of social criticism, and of "progessive" sociopolitical doctrine, as well as an emphasis on aesthetics, on finding one's "identity," on spontaneity in relationships, and on being antagonistic toward traditional authority, are likely to be found in the social sciences and the mind-studying trades, or espoused by their members, as well as by the liberal students. Consequently, when these scientists and clinicians undertake to evaluate today's left and/or drug-using students, they are often looking at people much like themselves. . . . These "liking" reactions probably reflect preferences for people acting more as . . . [the investigators] thought people ought to act. . . . The danger is that the evaluation may be positive only because of the charm of the young people without the investigators' recognizing the grounds for their reactions and without coming to grips with either fundaments or implications of student behavior. . . . The corollary danger is also acute and is commonplace. When conservative people offer their more negative evaluations of . . . radical students, many university and professionally based people reject outright what the "reactionaries" have to say [p. 377].

Just as many social scientists have erred, on the one hand, in their tendency to ignore contradictory evidence and to evaluate the student left in unrealistically positive terms, so, on the other hand, have many journalists and politicians erred in the close-minded extremity of their denunciations of student protestors as all bad, rebellious, maladjusted, and so forth. As Stinchcombe (1964) has put it: "One of the favorite substitutes for religion in a secular world is pontification on social problems without investigating them [p. 185]."

In like fashion, some social scientists have evaluated right-wing students very harshly, depicting them as not as intelligent or as adjusted as liberal students, even though there is much evidence to the contrary. As I have indicated above, I know of no investigators who have taken the mirror-image view that student rightists are extraordinarily adjusted or intellectually endowed.

It is time to recognize ideological differences for what they are—ideological differences—and not to infer that certain psychological qualities are necessarily related to those differences *without evidence for these inferences.* Everyone has his biases—social scientists, journalists, politicians, me— but it is one thing to have them, recognize them, and try to be objective about them by examining one's thinking and evaluation of evidence in the light of one's prejudices, and it is another to so let them direct one's work or thinking as to place the accuracy of that work and thinking into question. I would plead with political figures, journalists, social scientists particularly—with anyone who is moved to "pontificate" on this social phenomenon—to avoid making unsupported statements, for they only tend to polarize rather than to enlighten. I would further urge them to respect political and ideological differences for what they are, and not automatically to assume them to be reflections of personality disturbance or personality richness. If we do not do that, we engage in emotionally based "axiomatic" statements about those with whom we disagree politically or ideologically. Characterizing left activist youth as ". . . a social criminal class of self-appointed elitists . . . . which consists of spoiled brats who never had a good spanking [Spiro T. Agnew, quoted in Franklin, 1968, p. 74]" on the one hand, or on the other hand stating unequivocally in the face of so much contradictory evidence that "leftist views, statistically speaking mind you, are associated with better education, fewer neurotic tendencies, and so on, than rightist views—or even moderate, 'centrist' views [Bay, 1970, p. 86]" only generates heat, not light. If we are going to understand today's American college students—their attitudes, their values, their motivations, their goals, their actions, as well as their ideologies—we shall need not heat, but light.

References

Abramowitz, S. I. *The comparative competence-adjustment of student left social-political activists.* Unpublished doctoral dissertation, University of Colorado, 1972. [15, 105, 106, 117]

Adorno, T. W., Frenkel-Brunswik, E., Levinson, D. J., & Sanford, R. N. *The authoritarian personality.* New York: Harper, 1950. [42]

Astin, A. W. Personal and environmental determinants of student activism. *Measurement and Evaluation in Guidance,* 1968, 1, 149-161. [1, 2, 3, 17, 111]

Astin, A. W., & Bayer, A. E. Antecedents and consequents of disruptive campus protests. *Measurement and Evaluation in Guidance,* 1971, 4, 18-30. [75]

Bay, C. Political and apolitical students: Facts in search of theory. *Journal of Social Issues,* 1967, 23, 76-91. [1, 4, 11, 12, 14, 19, 20, 76, 80]

Bay, C. Political and apolitical students: Facts in search of theory. In E. E. Sampson, H. A. Korn, and Associates (Eds.), *Student activism and protest.* San Francisco: Jossey-Bass, 1970. Pp. 60-88. [125]

Bettelheim, B. Student revolt: The hard core. *Vital Speeches of the Day,* 1969, 35, 405-410. [1, 3, 20, 80]

Block, J., Haan, N., & Smith, M. B. Activism and apathy in contemporary adolescents. In J. F. Adams (Ed.), *Understanding adolescence: Current developments in adolescent psychology.* Boston: Allyn and Bacon, 1968. Pp. 198-231. [4, 7, 16, 117]

Blum, R. H. Epilogue: Students and drugs. In R. H. Blum (Ed.), *Drugs II: Students and drugs.* San Francisco: Jossey-Bass, 1969. Pp. 361-381. [123]

Borgatta, E. F., & Corsini, R. J. *Quick Word Test manual.* New York: Harcourt, Brace and World, 1964. [44, 77, 150]

Braungart, R. G. SDS and YAF: Backgrounds of student political activists. Paper presented at the meeting of the American Sociological Association, Miami, August 1966. [1, 7, 17, 60, 64, 67, 111]

Cowdry, R. W., Keniston, K., & Cabin, S. The war and military obligation: Private attitudes and public actions. *Journal of Personality,* 1970, 38, 525-549. [5, 7, 49, 59, 61, 97, 110]

. . . .

Numbers appearing in brackets after each reference refer to the text page number(s) where that reference was cited.

Dunlap, R. Radical and conservative student activists: A comparison of family backgrounds. *Pacific Sociological Review*, 1970, 13, 171-181. [7, 17]

Eisenhart, C., Hastay, M., & Wallis, W. A. (Eds.). *Techniques of statistical analysis*. New York: McGraw-Hill, 1947. [54]

Fellows at the Center for Advanced Study in the Behavioral Sciences. Student protests: A phenomenon for behavioral sciences research. *Science*, 1968, 161, 20-23. [2]

Feuer, L. S. *The conflict of generations: The character and significance of student movements*. New York: Basic Books, 1969. [20, 21, 69]

Flacks, R. The liberated generation: An exploration of the roots of student protest. *Journal of Social Issues*, 1967, 23, 52-75. [1, 8, 12, 17, 20, 131]

Franklin, B. A. Agnew deplores disorder in U.S. *New York Times*, September 29, 1968, 74. [125]

Geller, J. D., & Howard, G. Student activism and the war in Vietnam. Unpublished manuscript, Yale University, 1969. [12, 15, 16, 76, 110]

Gordon, L. V. *Manual for Survey of Interpersonal Values*. Chicago: Science Research Associates, 1960. [40, 83, 89, 93, 142]

Gordon, L. V. *Manual: Gordon Personal Profile*. (Rev. ed.) New York: Harcourt, Brace and World, 1963. (a) [41, 79, 89, 93, 95, 143]

Gordon, L. V. *Research briefs on Survey of Interpersonal Values*. Chicago: Science Research Associates, 1963. (b) [142]

Guilford, J. P., & Zimmerman, W. S. *The Guilford-Zimmerman Temperament Survey manual*. Beverly Hills, California: Sheridan Psychological Services, 1949. [44, 79, 89, 93, 95, 151]

Haan, N., Smith, M. B., & Block, J. Moral reasoning of young adults: Political-social behavior, family background, and personality correlates. *Journal of Personality and Social Psychology*, 1968, 10, 183-201. [7, 17, 105, 115, 116, 118]

Halleck, S. L. Hypotheses about student unrest. *Today's Education*, 1968, 57(6), 22-26. [3]

Harvey, W. R. *Least squares analysis of data with unequal subclass numbers*. (Publication ARS-20-8) Washington: United States Department of Agriculture, July 1960. [52]

Hedberg, R. More on forced-choice test fakability. *Journal of Applied Psychology*, 1962, 46, 125-127. [142]

Heist, P. Intellect and commitment: The faces of discontent. In O. A. Knorr and W. J. Minter (Eds.), *Order and freedom on the campus: The rights and responsibilities of faculty and students*. Boulder, Colorado: Western Interstate Commission on Higher Education, 1965. Pp. 61-70. [6, 8, 10, 11, 12, 13, 20]

Heist, P., & Yonge, G. *Omnibus Personality Inventory manual.* New York: Psychological Corporation, 1968. [6, 10, 14, 78]

Kahn, R. M., & Bowers, W. J. The social context of the rank-and-file student activist: A test of four hypotheses. *Sociology of Education,* 1970, 43, 38-55. [13, 17]

Katz, J. The student activists: Rights, needs, and powers of undergraduates. Report prepared for the United States Office of Education, 1967. [4, 6, 11, 12, 13, 20, 67, 76, 80, 119]

Katz, J. *No time for youth.* San Francisco: Jossey-Bass, 1968. [12]

Kelman, S. *Push comes to shove: The escalation of student protest.* Boston: Houghton-Mifflin, 1970. [118]

Keniston, K. The sources of student dissent. *Journal of Social Issues,* 1967, 23, 108-137. [11]

Keniston, K. *Young radicals: Notes on committed youth.* New York: Harcourt, Brace and World, 1968. [8, 15, 21, 98, 101, 117]

Keniston, K. Notes on young radicals. *Change,* 1969, 1, 25-33. [115, 116]

Kennan, G. Rebels without a program. *New York Times Magazine,* January 21, 1968. [1, 3]

Kerpelman, L. C. Personality and attitude correlates of political candidate preference. *Journal of Social Psychology.* 1968, **76,** 219-226. [43, 91, 144]

Kerpelman, L. C. Concurrent validity of a brief test of academic aptitude. *Educational and Psychological Measurement,* 1969, **29,** 891-894. (a) [141]

Kerpelman, L. C. Student political activism and ideology: Comparative characteristics of activists and nonactivists. *Journal of Counseling Psychology,* 1969, **16,** 8-13. (b) [7, 15, 43, 70, 74, 75, 80, 117, 133, 144, 146]

Knott, P. D. *Student activism.* Dubuque, Iowa: W. C. Brown, 1971. [118]

Lenin, V. I. *Collected Works.* Vol. 25. *June-September 1917.* Translated and edited by Stepan Apresyan and Jim Riordan. Moscow: Progress Publishers, 1964. [118]

Lenski, G. Status crystallization: A non-vertical dimension of social status. *American Sociological Review,* 1954, 19, 405-413. [21]

Leo, J. Studies agree that most campus activists are comparatively intelligent, stable and unprejudiced. *New York Times,* June 19, 1967, C29. [119].

Levinson, D. J. T. A. P. social attitude battery. Cambridge, Massachusetts: Harvard University, 1959. (Mimeographed) [42]

Lindquist, E. F. *Design and analysis of experiments in psychology and education.* Boston: Houghton-Mifflin, 1953. [55]

Lipset, S. M. The activists: A profile. *The Public Interest*, Fall 1968, 39-51. [7, 117]

Lipset, S. M. Dimensions of student involvement. In S. M. Lipset and G. Schaflander, *Passion and politics: Student activism in America.* Boston: Little-Brown, 1971. [62]

Lipset, S. M., & Altbach, P. Student politics and higher education in the United States. *Comparative Education Review,* 1966, 10, 320-349. [60]

Loken, J. O. A multivariate analysis of student activism at the University of Alberta. Unpublished doctoral dissertation, University of Alberta, 1970. [15]

Newfield, J. *A prophetic minority.* New York: New American Library, 1966. [1]

Peterson, R. E. *Technical manual, College Student Questionnaires.* Princeton, N.J.: Educational Testing Service, 1965. [40]

Peterson, R. E. *The scope of organized student protest in 1964-65.* Princeton, N.J.: Educational Testing Service, 1966. [17]

Peterson, R. E. Predictive validity of a brief test of academic aptitude. *Educational and Psychological Measurement,* 1968, 28, 441-444. (a) [77, 141]

Peterson, R. E. *The scope of organized student protest in 1967-68.* Princeton, N.J.: Educational Testing Service, 1968. (b) [2, 3, 17, 75]

Peterson, R. E. The student left in American higher education. *Daedalus,* 1968 (Winter), 293-317. (c) [1, 60]

Sampson, E. E. Student activism and the decade of protest. *Journal of Social Issues,* 1967, 23, 1-33. [3, 15, 20, 98, 101, 105, 117]

Schiff, L. F. The obedient rebels: A study of college conversions to conservatism. *Journal of Social Issues,* 1964, 20, 74-95. [97, 105]

Somers, R. H. The mainsprings of the rebellion: A survey of Berkeley students in November, 1964. In S. M. Lipset and S. S. Wolin (Eds.), *The Berkeley student revolt.* New York: Anchor, 1965. Pp. 530-537. [12, 76]

Stinchcombe, A. I. *Rebellion in a high school.* Chicago: Quadrangle Books, 1964. [124]

Trent, J. W., & Craise, J. L. Commitment and conformity in the American college. *Journal of Social Issues,* 1967, 23, 34-51. [6, 8, 10, 11, 13, 20, 76]

Veldman, D. J. *Fortran programming for the behavioral sciences.* New York: Holt, Rinehart and Winston, 1967. [57]

Walsh, J. ACE study on campus unrest: Questions for behavioral scientists. *Science,* 1969, 165, 157-160. [16]

Watts, W. A., Lynch, S., & Whittaker, D. Alienation and activism in today's college-age youth: Socialization patterns and current family relationships. *Journal of Counseling Psychology*, 1969, 16, 1-7. [14]

Watts, W. A., & Whittaker, D. Free speech advocates at Berkeley. *Journal of Applied Behavioral Science*, 1966, 2, 41-62. [8, 12, 67]

Westby, D. L., & Braungart, R. G. Class and politics in the family backgrounds of student political activists. *American Sociological Review*, 1966, 31, 690-692. [7]

Westby, D. L., & Braungart, R. G. Utopian mentality and conservatism: The case of the Young Americans for Freedom. Paper presented at the meeting of the American Sociological Association, San Francisco, August 1967. [7]

Westby, D. L., & Braungart, R. G. The alienation of generations and status politics: Alternative explanations of student political activism. In R. S. Sigel (Ed.), *Learning about politics: A reader in political socialization*. New York: Random House, 1970. Pp. 476-489. [7, 21, 22]

Whittaker, D., & Watts, W. A. Societal confrontation or withdrawal: Group personality contrasts of two extreme youth subcultures. Paper presented at the meeting of the Western Psychological Association, San Diego, March 1968. [80]

Whittaker, D., & Watts, W. A. Personality characteristics associated with activism and disaffiliation in today's college-age youth. *Journal of Counseling Psychology*, 1971, 18, 200-206. [11, 20, 96, 105]

Winborn, B. B., & Jansen, D. G. Personality characteristics of campus social-political action leaders. *Journal of Counseling Psychology*, 1967, 14, 509-513. [7, 15, 97]

Winer, B. J. *Statistical principles in experimental design*. New York: McGraw-Hill, 1962. [54]

Notes

Chapter 1

1. I have requested from Dr. Heist the numerical data upon which this finding was based, but unfortunately he has been unable to locate the original data. (Paul Heist. Personal communication, December 1969.)

2. Richard Flacks. Personal communication, December 1969. Flacks's own position (Personal communication, July 1970) is not that left activists are intellectually superior. Flacks (1967) was attempting to counter the notion, then existing in the popular media, that activists of the left were academic misfits by obtaining measures of their academic achievement. His data indicated that they were no different in this area than other student subgroups. Others have, however, carried this notion to the extreme to argue, as is now current in the scientific literature, that left activists are intellectually superior, citing Flacks's (1967) findings as support. Flacks's data neither indicate a clear difference in academic performance between left activists and other student subgroups, nor does Flacks claim that grade point average is a reflection of intelligence.

Chapter 3

1. The demonstrations referred to at the three institutions were of such intensity and the issues so national in scope as to warrant being reported in the national news media. This points up some of the unique problems encountered by the researcher who attempts to study student activism in vivo. In addition to dealing with administrators who feel that their institution's reputation might be harmed, and with students who, sometimes with past justification, are suspicious of the nature of the research and of the use to which it will be put, there are the practical problems of scheduling research appointments around planned demonstrations and counterdemonstrations that have the campus and the organizations in a turmoil, and of having to cancel, at the last minute, research appointments that were scheduled when spontaneous demonstrations occurred. The researcher must have a certain amount of flexibility and willingness to change plans in the face of events, and a sense of humor to sustain him through the trials and tribulations of attempting to gather meaningful data while important, yet disrupting, events are occurring.

2. The political science department faculty returns from Burgess were so scant that the prerating data could not be used in the selection of the target organizations at that institution, and consequently they are not reported here. At Burgess, I relied upon the consultant's knowledge of the campus organizations in approaching and selecting organizations to participate in the investigation. Since the preratings served the purpose only of ascertaining which organizations were likely to include students of a particular political ideology and did not serve as the final criterion of the political ideology of the students, target organizations at Burgess could be selected in the absence of preratings without vitiating the research results. The preratings were an extra nicety, in other words, and not an essential element in the research design.

3. Copies of Levinson's original T.A.P. instrument may be obtained from him at the Yale University of Medicine.

Chapter 5

1. Some additional anecdotal evidence supports the latter assumption, at least at one of the institutions. At Burgess University, several of the right activists came to the research appointment ostensibly as members of other groups, but they privately informed me that they were members of the right activist organization. When I inquired about the reason for this, they indicated that they feared for their physical safety if they were identified as members of the rightist group. I checked with my consultant on that campus, who confirmed that their fears were not entirely unrealistic, pointing out that one of the people had had his dormitory window shattered by a brick during a left activist demonstration.

2. There was some overlap in organization membership, but not to a marked degree. That is, some students belonged to both a student left organization and a student government organization on campus. This did not occur often. When it did, the students were asked, in the research session, to select the organization to which they gave more time and investment, and they were placed in that group for the purpose of the research.

Chapter 6

1. All the activist-nonactivist differences within an ideology group were consistently in the same direction, but the *magnitudes* of the

differences, while statistically significant, were not similar from ideology to ideology, thus accounting for the significant Activism X Ideology interaction in the analysis of variance.

2. These results provide, as well, further evidence in support of the validity of the Activity Scale.

3. My previous finding of a higher level of measured intellectual ability of all activists compared with all nonactivists in one institution of higher education (Kerpelman, 1969b) was not replicated in the present study. That finding perhaps resulted from the empirical confusion of both age and year level in school with the activism dimension (the activists were higher on both variables), a speculation that was put forth in the previous study. In any case, that study also failed to find an activism-ideology interaction effect on the variable of intelligence.

4. The subsample sizes for the GPP and for the GZTS differ from those of the other questionnaires. One middle nonactivist Camden student was dropped from the GPP data pool because he did not fill out that questionnaire completely. Many respondents, in many of the subgroups, were dropped from the various GZTS data pools because they marked too many items (four or more per scale) with a "?," making their scores on those scales unreliable. As a result, all of the GZTS data are based upon attenuated sample sizes, and they should be interpreted with this limitation in mind.

5. Statistical analyses of the Guilford-Zimmerman Temperament Survey Objectivity-Subjectivity Scale results at each institution for the significant analysis of variance interactions of Institution X Activism and Institution X Ideology revealed no significant effects. Apparently, the ideology differences and the activism differences at each institution for this Scale were consistently in the same direction, but the *magnitude* of the differences was neither statistically significant nor consistent.

6. All students who were arrested were arraigned the same night and released early the next morning on their own recognizance, so that none of them were still in jail when the research questionnaires were administered.

7. The first two roots were the only ones which yielded significant chi-squares. For Factor 1, $\chi^2 = 130.06$, $df = 21$, $p < .001$; Root 1 accounted for 63.33% of the variance. For Factor 2, $\chi^2 = 42.15$, $df = 19$, $p < .002$; this root accounted for 16.55% of the variance.

Chapter 7

1. The three 3-way analysis of variance interactions that resulted (on the SIV-C, SIV-I, and GZTS-O Scales) did delineate activism-ideology subgroup differences, but these differed among the institutions; there were no general activism-ideology trends that held across the three institutions.

2. This picture is, of course, overdrawn. There are many mass media and political commentators who are sympathetic to the student movement, just as there are social scientists who are disdainful of it. On the whole, however, I think the picture drawn is a fair one.

APPENDIX A
INFORMATION ON RESEARCH INSTRUMENTS

Covering Letter for Political Science Department Proratings

Memo to: Faculty members of the Political Science Department

From: Larry C. Kerpelman

Subject: Attached rating sheet

As a preliminary to studying the attitudinal factors that enter into political activity among college students, I need to obtain ratings on the political "character" of various political and social organizations. As a member of the Political Science Department, you may or may not feel that you are in a particularly advantageous position to provide these ratings. Your judgment, though, would provide the best "educated guess" that can be obtained on this campus, and accordingly I would like to have your judgment. The Chairman of the department has given his assent to this procedure; I wonder if I could prevail upon you to take a few minutes of your time to fill out the enclosed rating sheet. After you have completed it, would you kindly place it in the envelope provided and return it by Wednesday, October 30. Thank you for your cooperation.

> Larry C. Kerpelman
> Department of Psychology
> University of Massachusetts

CAMPUS ORGANIZATION RATING SHEET

(To be returned to ———— by Wednesday, October 30)

On the left-hand side of the page are names of various organizations on this campus. Across the top of the page are five column headings that could describe the political orientations of the organization. For each and every organization, please place a check mark under the column heading that most closely approximates your judgment of the political character of that organization. It is important that you assess each campus organization, even if you have little or no information about it and must guess. If you guess, make an "educated guess" based upon where you think the organization might stand. The two columns on the right-hand side are provided for you to indicate upon what you based your judgment.

Organization	Extremely politically liberal	Moderately politically liberal	Neither politically liberal nor politically conservative	Moderately politically conservative	Extremely politically conservative	Judgment based on:	
						Fair to good general information about the organization	Little or no general information about the organization

Code Number Instructions

Month of birth (Jan. = 01, ... Dec = 12)

Day of birth (1=01, 9=09, 10=10, 11=11, etc.)

Age now

Group code (To be provided by experimenter)

Membership (office or leader = 1, member only = 2)

Sex (male = 1, female = 2)

Year in school (freshman = 1, . . .
            senior = 4, graduate student = 5)

Number of years at this institution (If not student at
      this institution = 0)

Major (Refer to major list below and put in the 2-digit
      number that most closely describes your major)

Write in numbers with this side up (Top)

Agriculture = 01	Humanities = 07
Biological Sciences = 02	Natural Sciences = 08
Business = 03	Nursing = 09
Creative or Fine Arts = 04	Physical Sciences = 10
Education = 05	Social Sciences = 11
Engineering = 06	Other = 12

This code number will be used on all answer sheets to provide
an identification number unique to you. Consequently, it is
important that you fill in this code number carefully. After you
have completed your code number, turn this page around so
that the word Top is at the top. Then carefully fill in your code
number on each answer sheet that you will use as you come to
it.

Control Test AA

Moderate validity has been reported for the Control Test AA (CTAA). In a study of its predictive validity, Peterson (1968a) reported correlations between CTAA score and self-reported freshman grade point average of .39, .40, and .51, at an independent coeducational liberal arts college, an independent liberal arts college for Negro men, and a Roman Catholic liberal arts college for women, respectively. Kerpelman (1969a) reported a correlation between the same variables of .33 for students at a public coeducational university, and a correlation between CTAA scores and Wechsler Adult Intelligence Scale scores of .34 for similar students. In the research project reported in this book, the CTAA would be revealed to correlate with the Borgatta and Corsini Quick Word Test (described below) at coefficients of .25 at Smithvale, .57 at Burgess, and .47 at Camden.

Survey of Interpersonal Values

The Survey of Interpersonal Values (SIV) has been extensively investigated. Numerous studies of its factorial, criterion, and predictive validity have been reported by Gordon (1960, 1963b), most of which are supportive of the scale's validity. The SIV has been found, in addition, to be difficult for college students to fake. No significant differences were found among any of the scales when college students took the SIV twice at a two-week interval, once under simulated employment-seeking conditions and once under simulated guidance-seeking conditions (Hedberg, 1962). Furthermore, each item set is approximately equated for social desirability (Gordon, 1960). The SIV has been found to be relatively independent of intelligence, a desirable property if we do not want our measures to be confounded with intellectual ability. The SIV is negligibly correlated (−.22 to +.17) with the various scales of the College Qualification Test, a measure of intelligence among college students (Gordon, 1960). Reliability of the SIV with college students is moderately high, with Kuder-Richardson correlations for the six scales ranging from .71 to .86, and test-retest correlations over a ten-day interval ranging from .78 to .89 for the six scales (Gordon, 1960).

Gordon Personal Profile

Gordon (1963a) has reported numerous studies bearing upon the validity of the Gordon Personal Profile (GPP) in terms not only of face validity but also, and more importantly, of concurrent and predictive validity. The GPP has been found to be slightly more susceptible to "faking-good" than the Survey of Interpersonal Values, but the distortions are relatively small in magnitude. The GPP scales are negligibly correlated (-.23 to +.19) with various measures of aptitude and intelligence among college students (Gordon, 1963a), and so, like the Survey of Interpersonal Values, the Gordon Personal Profile is only slightly correlated with intellectual ability among college students. Reliability of the GPP with college students is moderately high, with split-half reliabilities for the four scales ranging from .84 to .88, Kuder-Richardson reliability coefficients ranging from .74 to .85, and test-retest (one week interval) reliabilities ranging from .84 to .87.

Politico-Economic Conservatism Scale

The construct validity of the Politico-Economic Conservatism Scale (PEC) has been supported in an investigation in which a general Liberal-Conservative factor loaded .89 on the PEC Scale in a discriminant pattern analysis (Kerpelman, 1968). The scale's criterion validity has been supported in a study in which a 3-point difference (out of a 6-point range) was found on the PEC Scale between left and right activist university students (Kerpelman, 1969b). The PEC Scale also has been demonstrated to have moderately high (.87) split-half reliability when administered to college students (Kerpelman, 1969b).

Politico-Economic Conservatism Scale

The statements below concern what the general public thinks about a number of social questions. The best answer to each statement below is *your personal opinion*. We have tried to cover many different points of view. You may find yourself agreeing strongly with some of the statements, disagreeing just as strongly with others, and perhaps uncertain about others. Whether you agree or disagree with any statement, you can be sure that many other people feel the same way that you do.

Record your answer to each statement by blackening in the appropriate space for the statement number according to how much you agree or disagree with it. Please answer every item. Blacken in +1, +2, +3, -1, -2, -3, depending on how you feel in each case.

+1: I AGREE A LITTLE	-1: I DISAGREE A LITTLE
+2: I AGREE PRETTY MUCH	-2: I DISAGREE PRETTY MUCH
+3: I AGREE VERY MUCH	-3: I DISAGREE VERY MUCH

1. When private enterprise does not do the job, it is up to the government to step in and meet the public's need for housing, water power, and the like.
2. Men like Henry Ford or J. P. Morgan, who overcame all competition on the road to success, are models for all young people to admire and imitate.
3. The government should own and operate all public utilities (railroads, gas and electricity, etc.).
4. In general, full economic security is bad; most men wouldn't work if they didn't need the money for eating and living.

5. The only way to do away with poverty is to make basic changes in our political and economic system.
6. There should be some upper limit, such as $100,000 per year, on how much any person can earn.
7. At this time, powerful "big unions" are a greater danger than powerful "big business" to our national welfare.
8. We need less government controls over business practices and profits.
9. Labor unions in large corporations should be given a larger part in deciding company policy.
10. The government should not participate in a program of health insurance and medical care.
11. America may not be perfect, but the American way has brought us about as close as human beings can get to a perfect society.
12. Strong labor unions are necessary if the workingman is to get greater security and a better standard of living.

(This version of the PEC Scale, modified by the author, is reprinted with the permission of Daniel J. Levinson.)

Activity Scale

The Activity S‹ e (ACT) was used initially in an earlier study, the results of which sugg ‹sted that the scale measures what it is purported to measure. In that research (Kerpelman, 1969b), college student activists of all ideologies were found to score significantly higher than student nonactivists on both ACT subscales. In the same investigation, high reliability for the Activity Scale was also found. Split-half reliabilities were .93 and .96 for the ACT-A and ACT-D subscales, respectively (Kerpelman, 1969b). An item analysis of the scale as administered in the previous study revealed six items that correlated only moderately with their subscale total scores, and as a result, those items (numbers 4, 9, 11, 16, 21, and 23) were revised slightly for the instrument used in this study.

Activity Scale (Larry C. Kerpelman and Michael J. Weiner)

DIRECTIONS

This is a survey for research purposes only, and as such, there are no right or wrong answers. We are seeking to measure students' experiences and expectations concerning certain general issues. Please read each question carefully and blacken in the appropriate space in the answer sheet according to the response that comes *most closely* to your actual state of affairs.

In the following questions the word "issues" refers solely to broad *political* and *social* issues on or off campus. Campus issues that have little or no broad political or social implications (such as support or protest of food service, grading practices, teaching practices) are *not* to be considered issues for the purposes of this inventory. Campus issues that *would* have broad political or social implications (such as support or protest of controversial speakers or films, controversial books in the library) are to be considered issues for the purposes of this inventory. Off-campus issues that have no broad political or social implications (such as support or protest of city or town tax policy, local school board appointments, etc.) are *not* to be considered issues for the purposes of this inventory. Off-campus issues that *would* have broad political or social implications (such as support or protest of U.S.

foreign policy, major election campaigns, etc.) *are* to be considered issues for the purposes of this inventory.

1. How many times in the past three years have you organized a group to support or protest a political or social issue?
   a) 0 times b) 1-2 times c) 3-4 times d) 5-6 times e) 7 or more times
2. How many times in the past three years have you led, or directly assisted in leading, an already organized group supporting or protesting a political or social issue?
   a) 0 times b) 1-2 times c) 3-4 times d) 5-6 times e) 7 or more times
3. How many times in the past three years have you participated in a group supporting or protesting a political or social issue?
   a) 0 times b) 1-2 times c) 3-4 times d) 5-6 times e) 7 or more times
4. How many times in the past three years have you engaged in an extended argument with anyone over a political or social issue?
   a) 0 times b) 1-2 times c) 3-4 times d) 5-6 times e) 7 or more times
5. How many times in the past three years have you addressed a formal audience (i.e., been a scheduled speaker) concerning a political or social issue?
   a) 0 times b) 1-2 times c) 3-4 times d) 5-6 times e) 7 or more times
6. Approximately how much time during the average day do you spend trying to convince others to support or protest political or social issues?
   a) less than 15 min. b) 15-30 min. c) 30 min.-1 hr. d) 1-2 hr. e) more than 2 hr.
7. Approximately how much time during the average day do you spend discussing political or social issues?
   a) less than 15 min. b) 15-30 min. c) 30 min.-1 hr. d) 1-2 hr. e) more than 2 hr.
8. How many times in the past three years have you written something (pamphlet, handout, etc.) designed specifically to either inform or convince other people concerning a political or social issue?
   a) 0 times b) 1-2 times c) 3-4 times d) 5-6 times e) 7 or more times
9. How many books during the average month do you read on political or social issues?
   a) 0 b) 1-2 c) 3-4 d) 5-6 e) 7 or more
10. How much time during the average day do you spend reading material, the bulk of which includes news, comment, or factual information on political or social issues?
    a) less than 15 min. b) 15-30 min. c) 30 min.-1 hr. d) 1-2 hr. e) more than 2 hr.
11. How many times during the average month do you attend meetings which have as their focus political or social issues?

a) 0 times b) 1-2 times c) 3-4 times d) 5-6 times e) 7 or more times
12. How many times in an average month do you go to hear scheduled
    speakers talking about political or social issues?
    a) 0 times b) 1-2 times c) 3-4 times d) 5-6 times e) 7 or more times

Imagine yourself as having been free from all financial, social, academic,
etc., responsibilities or any other commitments on your time during the
past three years. Answer the following questions in terms of *what you
would have liked to have done* if that were the case.

13. How many times in the last three years would you have liked to
    have organized a group to support or protest a political or social
    issue?
    a) 0 times b) 1-2 times c) 3-4 times d) 5-6 times e) 7 or more times
14. How many times in the last three years would you have liked to
    have led, or directly assisted in leading, an already organized group
    supporting or protesting a political or social issue?
    a) 0 times b) 1-2 times c) 3-4 times d) 5-6 times e) 7 or more times
15. How many times in the last three years would you have liked to
    have participated in a group supporting or protesting a political or
    social issue?
    a) 0 times b) 1-2 times c) 3-4 times d) 5-6 times e) 7 or more times
16. How many times in the last three years would you have liked to
    have engaged in an extended argument with anyone over a political
    or social issue?
    a) 0 times b) 1-2 times c) 3-4 times d) 5-6 times e) 7 or more times
17. How many times in the past three years would you have liked to
    have addressed a formal audience (i.e., been a scheduled speaker)
    concerning a political or social issue?
    a) 0 times b) 1-2 times c) 3-4 times d) 5-6 times e) 7 or more times
18. Approximately how much time during the average day would you
    like to spend convincing others to support or protest political or
    social issues?
    a) less than 15 min. b) 15-30 min. c) 30 min.-1 hr. d) 1-2 hr.
    e) more than 2 hr.
19. Approximately how much time during the average day would you
    like to spend discussing political or social issues?
    a) less than 15 min. b) 15-30 min. c) 30 min.-1 hr. d) 1-2 hr.
    e) more than 2 hr.
20. How many times during the past three years would you have liked
    to have written something (pamphlet, handout, etc.) designed
    specifically to either inform or convince other people concerning a
    political or social issue?
    a) 0 times b) 1-2 times c) 3-4 times d) 5-6 times e) 7 or more times

21. How many books during the average month would you have liked to have read on political or social issues?
    a) 0 b) 1-2 c) 3-4 d) 5-6 e) 7 or more
22. How much time during the average day would you like to spend reading material, the bulk of which includes news, comment, or factual information on political or social issues?
    a) less than 15 min. b) 15-30 min. c) 30 min.-1 hr. d) 1-2 hr. e) more than 2 hr.
23. How many times during the average month would you like to attend meetings which have as their focus political or social issues?
    a) 0 times b) 1-2 times c) 3-4 times d) 5-6 times e) 7 or more times
24. How many times in the average month would you like to go to hear a scheduled speaker talking about political or social issues?
    a) 0 times b) 1-2 times c) 3-4 times d) 5-6 times e) 7 or more times

(The Activity Scale is reprinted with the permission of Larry C. Kerpelman and Michael J. Weiner.)

Quick Word Test

Form Am, level 2, of the Quick Word Test (QWT) was standardized on a normative sample of college freshmen, and thus it enables fine differentiations in intelligence to be made even within such high intelligence groups. A concurrent validity study of the Quick Word Test among college freshmen yielded correlation coefficients ranging from .58 to .78 between the QWT and various scales of the ACE Linguistic Test (Borgatta and Corsini, 1964). An odd-even split-half reliability coefficient of .90 has also been reported for Form Am, level 2, of the QWT among college freshmen.

Guilford-Zimmerman Temperament Survey

The reliabilities of the five Guilford-Zimmerman Temperament Survey (GZTS) subscales used in this research based upon responses from college students, range from .75 to .87 (Guilford and Zimmerman, 1949). This is approximately the same range as the reliability coefficients of the other scales used in this research. Evidence on the validity of the GZTS subscales is mostly of a factorial nature and is not as clear-cut as that for the other instruments used in this research (Guilford and Zimmerman, 1949).

Campus Activities List

Code no.:

To help us assess the range of your interests, please list below *all* campus organizations (whether formal or informal) to which you belong.

1. _____
2. _____
3. _____
4. _____
5. _____
6. _____
7. _____
8. _____
9. _____
10. _____
11. _____
12. _____
13. _____
14. _____
15. _____
16. _____
17. _____
18. _____
19. _____
20. _____

APPENDIX B
ANALYSIS OF VARIANCE SUMMARY TABLES

Resocialization
An American Experiment

By, Daniel B. Kennedy, Ph.D.
Director
Criminal Justice Center
Macomb County Community
College

August Kerber, Ph.D.
Professor of Educational
Sociology
Wayne State University

This is the first critical, thorough examination of all programs aimed at altering human behavior and accomplishments. Specifically, this exceptional work considers and investigates resocialization in three institutional areas, in which literally billions of dollars and rigorous effort by hundreds of thousands of individuals are expended in both public and private institutions:

- Compensatory education
- Criminal rehabilitation
- Training for the hardcore unemployed

The conclusions are dramatic: Compensatory education programs have failed to significantly improve reading levels. Criminal rehabilitation has not reduced the 70% recidivism rate of the criminal population, and even after intensive training courses, the hardcore unemployed generally remain unemployed.

Each form of resocialization is considered separately and analyzed in research fashion. Definitions, history, extent and theories of resocialization in each institutional area is presented, followed by an analysis of its over-all efficacy.

1972

Paperbound, $4.95
Hardbound, $9.95

Death and the College Student

Editor,
Edwin S. Shneidman, Ph.D.
Neuropsychiatric Institute
University of California at Los Angeles

Always in the background of the protest and violence among youth on the college campuses in the last few years—over and above the Vietnam war and the draft—has been the topic of death. *Death and the College Student*, a timely volume of nineteen essays edited by a distinguished thanatologist, was written by college students (in a Harvard course on death and suicide). The varied contents include brilliant personal reflections, contemplations of contemporary death and discussions of the sequelae and remnants of death—youth talking to youth about life's most vital topic, reflecting the deep malaise of our time.

1972

TABLE 22. Summary of Institution × Activism × Ideology analyses of variance for demographic information.

Source of variation	df	Age		Year in school		Year at institution		Number of activities	
		MS	F	MS	F	MS	F	MS	F
Institution	2	23.29	11.39***	6.97	6.40**	4.73	3.64*	20.19	6.25**
Activism	1	12.71	6.22*	3.89	3.57	3.12	2.40	21.26	6.58*
Ideology	2	6.39	3.12*	1.53	1.41	0.48	0.37	4.02	1.24
Institution × Activism	2	0.15	0.07	0.02	0.02	0.68	0.53	6.29	1.95
Institution × Ideology	4	3.74	1.83	1.49	1.37	1.20	0.92	7.85	2.43*
Activism × Ideology	2	1.73	0.85	1.25	1.14	0.82	0.63	0.97	0.30
Institution × Activism × Ideology	4	0.50	0.24	0.32	0.30	0.61	0.47	6.03	1.87
Within	211	2.04		1.09		1.30		3.23	
Total	228								

*p < .05.
**p < .005.
***p < .001.

TABLE 23. Summary of Institution × Activism × Ideology analyses
of variance for activism measures.

Source of variation	df	ACT-A		ACT-D	
		MS	F	MS	F
Institution	2	221.77	4.93**	91.98	1.21
Activism	1	4406.20	98.01***	4578.61	60.08***
Ideology	2	1235.46	27.48***	1388.04	18.22***
Institution × Activism	2	48.93	1.09	82.52	1.08
Institution × Ideology	4	42.55	0.95	72.31	0.95
Activism × Ideology	2	203.43	4.53*	58.84	0.77
Institution × Activism × Ideology	4	50.18	1.12	118.43	1.55
Within	211	44.96		76.20	
Total	228				

*p < .05.
**p < .01.
***p < .001.

TABLE 24. Summary of Institution × Activism × Ideology analyses of variance for intellectual ability measures.

Source of variation	df	QWT		CTAA	
		MS	F	MS	F
Institution	2	1979.81	10.79*	171.02	22.28*
Activism	1	36.26	0.20	0.01	0.00
Ideology	2	226.22	1.23	2.45	0.32
Institution × Activism	2	332.61	1.81	2.72	0.35
Institution × Ideology	4	47.48	0.26	4.15	0.54
Activism × Ideology	2	86.91	0.47	11.58	1.51
Institution × Activism × Ideology	4	124.86	0.68	11.37	1.48
Within	211	183.47		7.68	
Total	228				

*p < .001.

TABLE 25. Summary of Institution × Activism × Ideology analyses of variance for emotional stability measures.

Source of variation	GPP-E			GZTS-E		
	df	MS	F	df	MS	F
Institution	2	19.37	0.54	2	16.71	0.50
Activism	1	4.33	0.12	1	33.06	0.98
Ideology	2	0.62	0.02	2	22.60	0.67
Institution × Activism	2	2.37	0.07	2	51.74	1.53
Institution × Ideology	4	72.99	2.02	4	14.90	0.44
Activism × Ideology	2	52.54	1.46	2	41.87	1.24
Institution × Activism × Ideology	4	72.53	2.01	4	33.51	0.99
Within	210	36.09		188	33.72	
Total	227			205		

TABLE 26. Summary of Institution × Activism × Ideology analyses of variance for social acceptance measures.

Source of variation	df	SIV-R		SIV-S		SIV-C		SIV-I	
		MS	F	MS	F	MS	F	MS	F
Institution	2	35.49	2.08	0.03	0.00	58.31	3.46*	5.54	0.-8
Activism	1	10.67	0.63	156.65	6.53*	29.45	1.75	31.69	1.02
Ideology	2	113.27	6.65***	55.60	2.32	164.09	9.73****	152.24	4.89**
Institution × Activism	2	61.99	3.64*	22.48	0.94	21.42	1.27	15.07	0.48
Institution × Ideology	4	5.95	0.35	22.56	0.94	44.03	2.61*	64.86	2.08
Activism × Ideology	2	25.99	1.53	53.83	2.24	29.70	1.76	1.15	0.04
Institution × Activism × Ideology	4	9.26	0.54	12.86	0.54	53.34	3.16*	74.40	2.39*
Within	211	17.03		23.99		16.86		31.16	
Total	228								

*p < .05.
**p < .01.
***p < .005.
****p < .001.

TABLE 27. Summary of Institution × Activism × Ideology analyses of variance for social regard measures.

Source of variation	GPP-S			GZTS-S			SIV-B		
	df	MS	F	df	MS	F	df	MS	F
Institution	2	3.06	0.07	2	74.89	1.66	2	31.51	1.15
Activism	1	169.27	3.97*	1	3.32	0.07	1	2.52	0.09
Ideology	2	11.38	0.27	2	54.81	1.21	2	460.09	16.81**
Institution × Activism	2	17.85	0.42	2	87.85	1.94	2	1.95	0.07
Institution × Ideology	4	94.89	2.23	4	82.47	1.82	4	25.64	0.94
Activism × Ideology	2	68.77	1.61	2	7.23	0.16	2	2.77	0.10
Institution × Activism × Ideology	4	87.98	2.06	4	87.07	1.92	4	16.42	0.60
Within	210	42.63		166	45.26		211	27.38	
Total	227			183			228		

*p < .05.
**p < .001.

TABLE 28. Summary of Institution × Activism × Ideology analyses of variance for ascendancy and assertiveness measures.

Source of variation	GPP-A			GZTS-A			SIV-L		
	df	MS	F	df	MS	F	df	MS	F
Institution	2	10.10	0.25	2	71.39	2.15	2	1.01	0.03
Activism	1	426.18	10.42***	1	366.66	11.05****	1	190.99	5.87*
Ideology	2	43.69	1.07	2	31.40	0.95	2	167.58	5.15**
Institution × Activism	2	7.78	0.19	2	7.12	0.21	2	64.58	1.99
Institution × Ideology	4	29.99	0.73	4	74.00	2.23	4	34.11	1.05
Activism × Ideology	2	71.43	1.75	2	6.19	0.19	2	63.06	1.94
Institution × Activism × Ideology	4	56.62	1.39	4	29.09	0.88	4	19.38	0.60
Within	210	40.89		178	33.18		211	32.52	
Total	227			195			228		

*p < .05.
**p < .01.
***p < .005.
****p < .001.

TABLE 29. Summary of Institution × Activism × Ideology analyses of variance for levelheadedness measures.

Source of variation	GPP-R			GZTS-R			GZTS-0		
	df	MS	F	df	MS	F	df	MS	F
Institution	2	14.69	0.39	2	45.74	2.37	2	90.38	2.93
Activism	1	16.66	0.44	1	15.07	0.78	1	46.80	1.54
Ideology	2	38.93	1.02	2	17.56	0.91	2	117.53	3.87*
Institution × Activism	2	55.44	1.45	2	25.33	1.31	2	134.94	4.44*
Institution × Ideology	4	48.77	1.28	4	10.61	0.55	4	103.78	3.42**
Activism × Ideology	2	37.95	1.00	2	44.70	2.32	2	51.93	1.71
Institution × Activism × Ideology	4	29.95	0.79	4	36.87	1.91	4	130.57	4.30***
Within	210	38.14		174	19.31		177	30.36	
Total	227			191			194		

*p < .05.
**p < .01.
***p < .005.